Stealing Sugar from the Castle

SELECTED POEMS,
1950 TO 2013

ROBERT BLY

Stealing Sugar from the Castle

SELECTED POEMS,

1950 TO 2013

W. W. NORTON & COMPANY

New York · London

Epigraph to "A Man and a Woman and a Blackbird": from "Thirteen Ways of Looking at a Blackbird" from *The Collected Poems of Wallace Stevens* by Wallace Stevens, copyright 1954 by Wallace Stevens and renewed 1982 by Holly Stevens. Used by permission of Alfred A. Knopf, a division of Random House, Inc. and Faber and Faber Ltd. Any third party use of this material, outside of this publication, is prohibited. Interested parties must apply directly to Random House, Inc. for permission.

For information about permission to reproduce selections from this book, write to Permissions, W. W. Norton & Company, Inc., 500 Fifth Avenue, New York, NY 10110

For information about special discounts for bulk purchases, please contact W. W. Norton Special Sales at specialsales@wwnorton.com or 800-233-4830

Manufacturing by Courier Westford
Book design by Chris Welch
Production manager: Julia Druskin

Library of Congress Cataloging-in-Publication Data

Bly, Robert.
[Poems. Selections]
Stealing sugar from the castle : selected poems, 1950 to 2013 / Robert Bly. — First edition.
pages ; cm
Includes index.
ISBN 978-0-393-24007-8 (hardcover)
I. Title.
PS3552.L9A6 2013
811'.54—dc23
 2013015476

W. W. Norton & Company, Inc.
500 Fifth Avenue, New York, N.Y. 10110
www.wwnorton.com

W. W. Norton & Company Ltd.
Castle House, 75/76 Wells Street, London W1T 3QT

1 2 3 4 5 6 7 8 9 0

For Ruth
My Darling, let's dance a step

Contents

THE LIGHT AROUND THE BODY, 1967, AND RELATED POEMS

THE TEETH MOTHER NAKED AT LAST, 1970-1972

THE POINT REYES POEMS, 1974, AND RELATED POEMS

SLEEPERS JOINING HANDS, 1973–1986

LOVING A WOMAN IN TWO WORLDS, 1978–1985, AND RELATED POEMS

THIS BODY IS MADE OF CAMPHOR AND GOPHERWOOD, 1973–1980

THE MAN IN THE BLACK COAT TURNS, 1980–1984

MEDITATIONS ON THE INSATIABLE SOUL, 1990–1994

MORNING POEMS, 1993–1997

POEMS FROM EATING THE HONEY OF WORDS, 1999

THE NIGHT ABRAHAM CALLED TO THE STARS, 2001

MY SENTENCE WAS A THOUSAND YEARS OF JOY, 2005

TALKING INTO THE EAR OF A DONKEY, 2011

NEW POEMS, 2012–2013

Acknowledgments

The poems in this volume previously appeared in the following collections: *Silence in the Snowy Fields*, Wesleyan University Press, 1962; *The Light Around the Body*, Harper and Row, 1967; *The Morning Glory*, Kayak Books, 1969; *The Teeth Mother Naked at Last*, City Lights, 1970; *Sleepers Joining Hands*, Harper and Row, 1973; *The Point Reyes Poems*, Mudra, 1974; *The Morning Glory* (enlarged edition), Harper and Row, 1975; *This Body Is Made of Camphor and Gopherwood*, Harper and Row, 1977; *This Tree Will Be Here for a Thousand Years*, Harper and Row, 1979, revised 1992; *The Man in the Black Coat Turns*, Dial Press, 1981; *Loving a Woman in Two Worlds*, Dial Press, 1985; *Selected Poems*, Harper and Row, 1986; *Angels of Pompeii*, Ballantine, 1991; *What Have I Ever Lost by Dying?*, HarperCollins, 1992; *Meditations on the Insatiable Soul*, HarperCollins, 1994; *Morning Poems*, HarperCollins, 1997; *Eating the Honey of Words: New and Selected Poems*, HarperCollins, 1999; *The Night Abraham Called to the Stars*, HarperCollins, 2001; *My Sentence Was a Thousand Years of Joy*, HarperCollins, 2005; *Talking into the Ear of a Donkey*, W. W. Norton, 2011.

My grateful acknowledgment to the editors of the following publications in which the new poems in this volume were published:

American Poetry Review: "Love of the Wind"; "It's Not to Worry"
Chrysalis Reader: "It Takes a Long Time"

Clifden 35: The Clifden Anthology: *"Harmonium"*
Great River Review: "Tomas Tranströmer and the Human Ear"
Poetry Ireland Review: "My Father at Dawn"
Sufi: "Listening to Monteverdi"; "Plan for a Year"

And thanks to Thomas R. Smith for constant help and inspiration.

EARLY POEMS

1950–1955

A Home in Dark Grass

In the deep fall the body awakes
And we find lions on the seashore—
Nothing to fear.
The wind rises; the water is born,
Spreading white tomb-clothes on a rocky shore,
Drawing us up
From the bed of the land.

We did not come to remain whole.
We came to lose our leaves like the trees,
Trees that start again,
Drawing up from the great roots.
So men captured by the Moors
Wake rowing in the cold ocean
Air, living a second life.

That we should learn of poverty and rags,
That we should taste the weed of Dillinger,
And swim in the sea,
Not always walking on dry land,
And, dancing, find in the trees a savior,
A home in dark grass,
And nourishment in death.

When the Dumb Speak

There's a joyful night in which we lose
Everything, and drift
Like a radish
Rising and falling, and the ocean at last
Throws us into the ocean;
In that ocean we are sinking
As if floating on darkness.
The body raging,
And driving itself, disappearing in smoke:
Walks in large cities late at night,
Reading the Bible in Christian Science windows,
Or reading a history of Bougainville:
Then the images appear—
Images of grief,
Images of the body shaken in the grave,
And the graves filled with seawater;
Fires in the sea,
Bodies smoldering like ships,
Images of wasted life,
Life lost, imagination ruined,
The house fallen,
The gold sticks broken!
Then shall the talkative be silent
And the dumb will speak.

Where We Must Look for Help

The dove returns; it found no resting place;
It was in flight all night above the shaken seas.
Beneath Ark eaves
The dove shall magnify the tiger's bed;
Give the dove peace.
The split-tail swallows leave the sill at dawn;
At dusk blue swallows shall return.
On the third day the crow shall fly;
The crow, the crow, the spider-colored crow,
The crow shall find new mud to walk upon.

Awakening

We are approaching sleep: the chestnut blossoms in the mind
Mingle with thoughts of pain,
And the long roots of barley, bitterness
As of the oak roots staining the water dark
In Louisiana, the wet streets soaked with rain
And sodden blossoms, out of this
We have come, a tunnel softly hurtling into darkness.

The storm is coming. The small farmhouse in Minnesota
Is hardly strong enough for the storm.
Darkness, darkness in the grasses, darkness in trees.
Even the water in wells trembles.
Bodies give off darkness, and chrysanthemums
Are dark, and horses, who are bearing great loads of hay
To the deep barns where the dark air is moving from the corners.

Lincoln's statue, and the traffic. From the long past
Into the long present
A bird forgotten in these pressures, warbling,
As the great wheel turns around, grinding
The living in water.
Washing, continual washing, in water now stained
With blossoms and rotting logs, cries half-
Muffled, from beneath the earth, the living finally as awake as the dead.

SILENCE IN THE SNOWY FIELDS

1958–1978

and Related Poems

Waiting for Night to Come

I

How much I long for the night to come
Again—I am restless all afternoon—
And the huge stars to appear
All over the heavens! . . . The black spaces between stars . . .
And the blue to fade away.

II

I worked on poems with my back to the window,
Waiting for the darkness that I remember
Noticing from my cradle.
When I step over and open the door, I am
A salmon slipping over the gravel into the ocean.

III

One star stands alone in the western darkness:
Arcturus. Caught in their love, the Arabs called it
The Keeper of Heaven. I think
It was in the womb that I received
The thirst for the dark heavens.

Night

I

If I think of a horse wandering about sleeplessly
All night on this short grass covered with moonlight,
I feel a joy, as if I had thought
Of a pirate ship plowing through dark flowers.

II

The box elders around us are full of joy,
Obeying what is beneath them.
The lilacs are sleeping, and the plants are sleeping;
Even the wood made into a casket is asleep.

III

The butterfly is carrying loam on its wings;
The toad is bearing tiny bits of granite in his skin.
The leaves at the crown of the tree are asleep
Like the dark bits of earth at its root.

IV

Alive we are like a sleek black water beetle,
Skating across still water in any direction
We choose, and soon to be swallowed
Suddenly from beneath.

Snowfall in the Afternoon

I

The grass is half covered with snow.
It was the sort of snowfall that starts in late afternoon,
And now the little houses of the grass are growing dark.

II

If I could reach down, near the earth,
I could take handfuls of darkness!
A darkness that was always there, which we never noticed.

III

As the snow grows heavier, the cornstalks fade farther away,
And the barn moves nearer to the house.
The barn moves all alone in the growing storm.

IV

The barn is full of corn, and moving toward us now,
Like a hulk blown toward us in a storm at sea;
All the sailors on deck have been blind for many years.

Late at Night During a Visit of Friends

I

We spent all day fishing and talking.
At last, late at night, I sit at my desk alone,
And rise and walk out in the summery night.
A dark thing hopped near me in the grass.

II

The trees were breathing, the windmill slowly pumped.
Overhead the rain clouds that rained on Ortonville
Covered half the stars.
The air was still cool from their rain.

III

It is very late.
I am the only one awake.
Men and women I love are sleeping nearby.

IV

The human face shines as it speaks of things
Near itself, thoughts full of dreams.
The human face shines like a dark sky
As it speaks of those things that oppress the living.

Old Boards

I

I love to see boards lying on the ground in early spring:
The ground beneath them is wet, and muddy—
Perhaps covered with chicken tracks—
And they are dry and eternal.

II

This is the wood one sees on the decks of ocean ships,
Wood that carries us far from land,
With a dryness of something used for simple tasks,
Like a horse's tail.

III

This wood is like a man who has a simple life,
Living through the spring and winter on the ship of his own desire.
He sits on dry wood surrounded by half-melted snow
As the rooster walks away springily over the dampened hay.

Surprised by Evening

There is unknown dust that is near us,
Waves breaking on shores just over the hill,
Trees full of birds that we have never seen,
Nets drawn down with dark fish.

The evening arrives; we look up and it is there,
It has come through the nets of the stars,
Through the tissues of the grass,
Walking quietly over the asylums of the waters.

The day shall never end, we think:
We have hair that seems born for the daylight;
But, at last, the quiet waters of the night will rise,
And our skin shall see far off, as it does underwater.

Three Kinds of Pleasures

I

Sometimes, riding in a car, in Wisconsin
Or Illinois, you notice those dark telephone poles
One by one lift themselves out of the fence line
And slowly leap on the gray sky—
And past them, the snowy fields.

II

The darkness drifts down like snow on the picked cornfields
In Wisconsin: and on these black trees
Scattered, one by one,
Through the winter fields—
We see stiff weeds and brownish stubble,
And white snow left now only in the wheeltracks of the combine.

III

It is a pleasure, also, to be driving
Toward Chicago, near dark,
And see the lights in the barns.
The bare trees more dignified than ever,
Like a fierce man on his deathbed,
And the ditches along the road half full of a private snow.

After Drinking All Night with a Friend, We Go Out in a Boat at Dawn to See Who Can Write the Best Poem

These pines, these fall oaks, these rocks,
This water dark and touched by wind—
I am like you, you dark boat,
Drifting over water fed by cool springs.

Beneath the waters, since I was a boy,
I have dreamt of strange and dark treasures,
Not of gold or strange stones, but the true
Gift, beneath the pale lakes of Minnesota.

This morning also, drifting in the dawn wind,
I sense my hands, and my shoes, and this ink—
Drifting, as all of the body drifts,
Above the clouds of the flesh and the stone.

A few friendships, a few dawns, a few glimpses of grass,
A few oars weathered by the snow and the heat,
So we drift toward shore, over cold waters,
No longer caring if we drift or go straight.

Poem in Three Parts

I

Oh, on an early morning I think I shall live forever!
I am wrapped in my joyful flesh,
As the grass is wrapped in its clouds of green.

II

Rising from a bed, where I dreamt
Of long rides past castles and hot coals,
The sun lies happily on my knees;
I have suffered and survived the night
Bathed in dark water, like any blade of grass.

III

The strong leaves of the box elder tree,
Plunging in the wind, call us to disappear
Into the wilds of the universe,
Where we shall sit at the foot of a plant,
And live forever, like the dust.

Driving to Town Late to Mail a Letter

It is a cold and snowy night. The main street is deserted.
The only things moving are swirls of snow.
As I lift the mailbox door, I feel its cold iron.
There is a privacy I love in this snowy night.
Driving around, I will waste more time.

Driving Toward the Lac Qui Parle River

I

I am driving; it is dusk; Minnesota.
The stubble field catches the last growth of sun.
The soybeans are breathing on all sides.
Old men are sitting before their houses on car seats
In the small towns. I am happy,
The moon rising above the turkey sheds.

II

The small world of the car
Plunges through the deep fields of the night,
On the road from Willmar to Milan.
This solitude covered with iron
Moves through the fields of night
Penetrated by the noise of crickets.

III

Nearly to Milan, suddenly a small bridge,
And water kneeling in the moonlight.
In small towns the houses are built right on the ground;
The lamplight falls on all fours in the grass.
When I reach the river, the full moon covers it;
A few people are talking low in a boat.

Love Poem

When we are in love, we love the grass,
And the barns, and the lightpoles,
And the small main streets abandoned all night.

Taking the Hands

Taking the hands of someone you love,
You see they are delicate cages . . .
Tiny birds are singing
In the secluded prairies
And in the deep valleys of the hands.

After Working

I

After many strange thoughts,
Thoughts of distant harbors, and new life,
I came in and found the moonlight lying on the floor.

II

Outside it covers the trees like pure sound,
The sound of tower bells, or of water moving under the ice,
The sound of the deaf hearing through the bones of their heads.

III

We know the road; as the moonlight
Lifts everything, so in a night like this
The road goes on ahead, it is all clear.

Depression

I felt my heart beat like an engine high in the air,
Like those scaffolding engines standing only on planks;
My body hung about me like an old grain elevator,
Useless, clogged, full of blackened wheat.
My body was sour, my life dishonest, and I fell asleep.

I dreamt that men came toward me, carrying thin wires;
The wires, like fire, passed in; the men were old Tibetans,
Dressed in padded clothes, to keep out cold;
Then three work gloves, lying fingers to fingers,
In a circle, came toward me, and I awoke.

Now I want to see nothing more than two feet high.
I want to meet no one; I want to say nothing;
I want to go down and rest in the black earth of silence.

The Moon

After writing poems all day,
I go off to see the moon in the pines.
Far in the woods I sit down against a pine.
The moon has her porches turned to face the light,
But the deep part of her house is in darkness.

Thinking of Tu Fu's Poem

I get up late and ask what has to be done today.
Nothing has to be done, so the farm looks doubly good.
The blowing maple leaves fit so well with the moving grass,
The shadow of my writing shack looks small beside the growing trees.

Never be with your children, let them get stringy like radishes!
Let your wife worry about the lack of money!
Your whole life is like a drunkard's dream!
You haven't combed your hair for a whole month!

Winter Privacy Poems at the Shack

I

About four, a few flakes.
I empty the teapot out in the snow,
Feeling shoots of joy in the new cold.
By nightfall, wind;
The curtains on the south sway softly.

II

My shack has two rooms; I use one.
The lamplight falls on my chair and table,
And I fly into one of my own poems—
I can't tell you where—
As if I appeared where I am now,
In a wet field, snow falling.

III

More of the fathers are dying each day.
It is time for the sons.
Bits of darkness are gathering around them.
The darkness appears as flakes of light.

IV

Listening to Bach's Cello Concerto

Inside this music there is someone
Who is not well-described
By the names of Jesus, or Jehovah, or the Lord of Hosts.

V

There is a solitude like black mud!
Sitting in the darkness singing,
I can't tell if this joy
Is from the body, or the soul, or a third place!

VI

When I wake, new snow has fallen,
I am alone, yet someone else is with me,
Drinking coffee, looking out at the snow.

Passing an Orchard by Train

Grass high under apple trees.
The bark of the trees rough and sexual,
The grass growing heavy and uneven.

We cannot bear disaster, like
The rocks—
Swaying nakedly
In open fields.

One slight bruise and we die!
I know no one on this train.
A man comes walking down the aisle.
I want to tell him
That I forgive him, that I want him
To forgive me.

THE LIGHT AROUND THE BODY

1967

and Related Poems

But when this had given me many a hard blow, doubtless from the Spirit that had a desire for me, I finally fell into great sadness and melancholy, when I viewed the great depth of this world, the sun and the stars and the clouds, rain and snow, and contemplated in my mind the whole creation of this world.

So then I found in all things good and evil, love and wrath, in creatures of reason as well as in wood, in stone, in earth, in the elements, in men and animals. Withal, I considered the little spark "man" and what it might be esteemed to be by God in comparison with this great work of heaven and earth.

In consequence I grew very melancholy, and what is written, though I knew it well, could not console me.

—*Jacob Boehme*

Calling to the Badger

Come, let us write of Niagara and the Huron squaws,
The Puritans with their black robes, Dillinger
Like a dark wind. Bring in the advertising men,
So that the strong-haunched woman
By the blazing stove of the sun, the moon,
May come home to us, sitting on the naked wood
In another world, and all the Shell stations folded in a faint light.

Come, let us write of the sadness of the Indian fighters,
The sadness that rises from the death of the Diggers,
From the death of Logan alone in his house,
And the Cherokees forced to eat the tail of the Great Bear.
The old are being driven to Florida
Like Geronimo, and young men are still calling to the badger
And the otter, alone on the mountains of South Dakota.

Sleet Storm on the Merritt Parkway

I look out at the white sleet covering the still streets
As we drive through Scarsdale—
The sleet began falling as we left Connecticut,
And the winter leaves swirled in the wet air after cars
Like hands suddenly turned over in a conversation.
Now the frost has nearly buried the short grass of March.
Seeing the sheets of sleet untouched on the wide streets,
I think of the many comfortable homes stretching for miles,
Two and three stories, solid, with polished floors,
With white curtains in the upstairs bedrooms,
And small perfume flagons of black glass on the windowsills,
And warm bathrooms with guest towels, and electric lights—
What a magnificent place for a child to grow up!
And yet the children end in the river of price-fixing,
Or in the snowy field of the insane asylum.
The sleet falls—so many cars moving toward New York—
Last night we argued about the Marines invading Guatemala in 1947,
The United Fruit Company had one water spigot for two hundred
 families,
And the ideals of America, our freedom to criticize,
The slave systems of Rome and Greece, and no one agreed.

The Executive's Death

Merchants have multiplied more than the stars of heaven.
Half the population are like the long grasshoppers
That sleep in the bushes in the cool of the day:
The sound of their wings is heard at noon, muffled, near the earth.
The crane handler dies, the taxi driver dies, slumped over
In his taxi. Meanwhile, high in the air, an executive
Walks on the cool floor, and suddenly falls.
He dreams he is lost in a snowstorm in a mountain,
On which he crashed, carried at night by great machines.
As he lies on the wintery slope, cut off and dying,
A pine stump talks to him of Goethe and Jesus.
Commuters arrive in Hartford at dusk like moles
Or hares flying from a fire behind them,
And the dusk in Hartford is full of their sighs;
Their trains come through the air like a dark music,
Like the sound of horns, the sound of thousands of small wings.

Come with Me

Come with me into those things that have felt this despair for so long—
Those removed Chevrolet wheels that howl with a terrible loneliness,
Lying on their backs in the cindery dirt, like men drunk and naked,
Staggering off down a hill at night to drown at last in a pond.
Those shredded inner tubes abandoned on the shoulders of thruways,
Black and collapsed bodies, that tried and burst, and were left behind.
And those curly steel shavings, scattered about on garage benches,
Sometimes still warm, gritty when we hold them,
Who have given up, and blame everything on the government;
And those roads in South Dakota that feel around in the darkness . . .

Written in Dejection near Rome

What if these long races go on repeating themselves
Century after century, living in houses painted light colors
On the beach,
Black spiders,
Having turned pale and fat,
Men walking thoughtfully with their families,
Vibrations
Of exhausted violin-bodies,
Horrible eternities of sea pines!
Some men cannot help but feel it,
They will abandon their homes
To live on rafts tied together on the ocean;
Those on shore will go inside tree trunks,
Surrounded by bankers whose fingers have grown long and slender,
Piercing through rotting bark for their food.

As the Asian War Begins

There are longings to kill that cannot be seen,
Or are seen only by a minister who no longer believes in God,
Living in his parish like a crow in its nest.

And there are flowers with murky centers,
Impenetrable, ebony, basalt . . .

Conestogas go past, over the Platte, their contents
Hidden from us, murderers riding under the canvas . . .

Give us a glimpse of what we cannot see,
Our enemies, the soldiers and the poor.

Counting Small-Boned Bodies

Let's count the bodies over again.

If we could only make the bodies smaller,
The size of skulls,
We could make a whole plain white with skulls in the moonlight!

If we could only make the bodies smaller,
Maybe we could get
A year's kill in front of us on a desk!

If we could only make the bodies smaller,
We could fit
A body into a finger-ring, for a keepsake forever.

Hatred of Men with Black Hair

I hear voices praising Tshombe, and the Portuguese
In Angola, these are the men who skinned Little Crow!
We are all their sons, skulking
In back rooms, selling nails with trembling hands!

We distrust every person on earth with black hair;
We send teams to overthrow Chief Joseph's government;
We train natives to kill presidents with blowdarts;
We have men loosening the nails on Noah's Ark.

The State Department floats in the heavy jellies near the bottom
Like exhausted crustaceans, like squids who are confused,
Sending out beams of black light to the open sea,
Fighting their fraternal feeling for the great landlords.

We have violet rays that light up the jungles at night, showing
The friendly populations; we are teaching the children of ritual
To overcome their longing for life, and we send
Sparks of black light that fit the holes in the generals' eyes.

Underneath all the cement of the Pentagon
There is a drop of Indian blood preserved in snow:
Preserved from the trail of blood that once led away
From the stockade, over the snow, the trail now lost.

Johnson's Cabinet Watched by Ants

1.

It is a clearing deep in a forest: overhanging boughs
Make a low place. Here citizens we know during the day,
The ministers, the department heads,
Appear changed: the stockholders of large steel companies
In small wooden shoes: Here are the generals dressed as gamboling
 lambs.

2.

Tonight they burn the rice supplies; tomorrow
They lecture on Thoreau; tonight they move around the trees,
Tomorrow they pick the twigs from their clothes;
Tonight they throw the firebombs, tomorrow
They read the Declaration of Independence; tomorrow they are in
 church.

3.

Ants are gathered around an old tree.
In a choir they sing, in harsh and gravelly voices,
Old Etruscan songs on tyranny.
Toads nearby clap their small hands, and join
The fiery songs, their five long toes trembling in the soaked earth.

THE TEETH MOTHER NAKED AT LAST

1970–1972

The Teeth Mother Naked at Last

1.

Massive engines lift beautifully from the deck.
Wings appear over the trees, wings with eight hundred rivets.

Engines burning a thousand gallons of gasoline a minute sweep over
 the huts with dirt floors.

The chickens feel the new fear deep in the pits of their beaks.
Buddha with Padmasambhava.

Meanwhile, out on the China Sea,
Immense gray bodies are floating,
Born in Roanoke,
The ocean on both sides expanding, "buoyed on the dense marine."

Helicopters flutter overhead. The death-
Bee is coming. Super Sabres
Like knots of neurotic energy sweep
Around and return.
This is Hamilton's triumph.
This is the advantage of a centralized bank.
B-52s come from Guam. All the teachers
Die in flames. The hopes of Tolstoy fall asleep in the ant heap.
Do not ask for mercy.

Now the time comes to look into the past-tunnels,
The hours given and taken in school,
The scuffles in coatrooms,

Foam leaps from his nostrils,
Now we come to the scum you take from the mouths of the dead,
Now we sit beside the dying, and hold their hands, there is hardly
 time for goodbye.
The staff sergeant from North Carolina is dying—you hold his hand,
He knows the mansions of the dead are empty, he has an empty place
Inside him, created one night when his parents came home drunk.
He uses half his skin to cover it,
As you try to protect a balloon from sharp objects . . .

Artillery shells explode. Napalm canisters roll end over end.
Eight hundred steel pellets fly through the vegetable walls.
The six-hour infant puts his fists instinctively to his eyes to keep out
 the light.
But the room explodes;
The children explode;
Blood leaps on the vegetable walls.

Yes, I know, blood leaps on the walls—
Don't cry at that—
Do you cry at the wind pouring out of Canada?
Do you cry at the reeds shaken at the edge of the sloughs?
The Marine battalion enters.
This happens when the seasons change,
This happens when the leaves begin to drop from the trees too early
"Kill them: I don't want to see anything moving."
This happens when the ice begins to show its teeth in the ponds.
This happens when the heavy layers of lake water press down on the
 fish's head, and send him deeper, where his tail swirls slowly, and

his brain passes him pictures of heavy reeds, of vegetation fall on
vegetation . . .

2.

Excellent Roman knives slip along the ribs.

A stronger man starts to jerk up the strips of flesh.

"Let's hear it again, you believe in the Father, the Son, and the Holy Ghost?"

A long scream unrolls.

More.

*"From the political point of view, democratic institutions are being built in
Vietnam, wouldn't you agree?"*

A green parrot shudders under the fingernails.
Blood jumps in the pocket.
The scream lashes like a tail.

"Let us not be deterred from our task by the voices of dissent . . ."

The whines of the jets
Pierce like a long needle.

3.

It is a desire to eat death,
To gobble it down,
To rush on it like a cobra with mouth open.
It is a desire to take death inside,
To feel it burning inside, pushing out velvety hairs,
Like a clothes brush in the intestines—

That is the thrill that leads the President on to lie.

Now the Chief Executive enters, and the press conference begins.
First the President lies about the date the Appalachian Mountains rose.
Then he lies about the population of Chicago.
Then the number of fish taken every year in the Arctic,
Then about the weight of the adult eagle, then about the acreage of
 the Everglades.
He has learned the true birthplace of Attila the Hun,
Then he lies about the composition of the amniotic fluid.
He has private information about which city *is* the capital of Wyoming.

He insists that Luther was never a German,
And declares that only the Protestants sold indulgences,
That Pope Leo X *wanted* to reform the Church, but the liberal
 elements prevented him.
That the Peasants' War was fomented by Italians from the North.
And the Attorney General lies about the time the sun sets.

4.

These lies mean we have a longing to die.
What is there now to hold us on earth?
It is the longing for someone to come and take us by the hand to
 where they are all sleeping:
Where the Egyptian pharaohs are asleep, and our own mothers,
And all those disappeared children, who went around with us on
 the rings at grade school.

Do not be angry at the President—
He is longing to take in his hands the locks of death-hair:
To meet his own children, dead, or never born . . .

He is drifting sideways toward the dusty places.

5.

This is what it's like to watch the altimeter needle going mad

Baron 25, this is 81. Are there any friendlies in the area? 81 from 25,
 negative on the friendlies. I'd like you to take out as many structures as
 possible located in those trees within two hundred meters east and west of
 my smoke mark.

diving, the green earth swinging, cheeks hanging back, red pins
 blossoming ahead of us, 20-millimeter cannon fire, leveling off,
 rice fields shooting by like telephone poles, smoke rising, hut

roofs loom up huge as landing fields, slugs going in, half the huts
on fire, small figures running, palm trees burning, shooting past,
up again; . . . blue sky . . . cloud mountains . . .

This is what it's like to have a gross national product.

It is because we have so few women sobbing in back rooms,
Because we have so few children's heads torn apart by high-velocity
 bullets,
Because we have so few tears falling on our own hands
That the Super Sabre turns and screams down toward the earth.

6.

A car is rolling toward a rock wall.
The treads in the face begin to crack.
We feel like tires being run down roads under heavy cars.

The teenager imagines herself floating through the Seven Spheres.
Oven doors are found
Open.
Soot collects over the doorframe, has children, takes courses, goes
 mad, and dies.

7.

I know that books are tired of us.
I know they are chaining the Bible to chairs.
Books don't want to remain in the same room with us anymore.
New Testaments are escaping . . . dressed as women . . . they slip out
 after dark.
And Plato! Plato . . . Plato
Wants to hurry back up the river of time,
So he can end as a blob of seaflesh rotting on an Australian beach.

8.

Why are they dying? I have written this so many times.
They are dying because the President has opened a Bible again.
They are dying because gold deposits have been found among the
 Shoshoni Indians.

They are dying so that the mountain shadows will continue to fall
 east in the afternoon,
So that the beetle can move along the ground near the fallen twigs.

9.

But if one of those children came near that we have set on fire,
Came toward you like a gray barn, walking,
You would howl like a wind tunnel in a hurricane,
You would tear at your shirt with blue hands,
You would drive over your own child's wagon trying to back up,
The pupils of your eyes would go wild—

If a child came by burning, you would dance on a lawn,
Trying to leap into the air, digging into your cheeks,
You would ram your head against the wall of your bedroom
Like a bull penned too long in his moody pen—

If one of those children came toward me with both hands
In the air, fire rising along both elbows,
I would suddenly go back to my animal brain,
I would drop on all fours, screaming,
My vocal cords would turn blue; so would yours;
It would be a month before I could play with my own children again.

10.

I want to sleep awhile in the rays of the sun slanting over the snow.
Don't wake me.
Don't tell me how much grief there is in the leaf with its natural oils.
Don't tell me how many children have been born with stumpy hands
All those years we lived in St. Augustine's shadow.

Tell me about the dust that falls from the yellow daffodil shaken in
the restless winds.
Tell me about the particles of Babylonian thought that still pass
through the earthworm every day.
Don't tell me about "the frightening laborers who do not read books."

Now the whole nation starts to whirl,
The end of the Republic breaks off,
Europe comes to take revenge,
The mad beast covered with European hair rushes toward the mesa
bushes in Mendocino County.
Pigs rush toward the cliff.
The waters underneath part: in one ocean luminous globes float up
(in them hairy and ecstatic men);
In the other ocean—the Teeth Mother, naked at last.

Let us drive cars
Up
The light beams
To the stars . . .

Then return to earth crouched inside the drop of sweat
That falls
From the chin of the Protestant tied in the fire.

THE POINT REYES POEMS

1974

and Related Poems

November Day at McClure's Beach

Alone on the jagged rock at the south end of McClure's Beach. The sky low. The sea grows more and more private, as afternoon goes on; the sky comes down closer; the unobserved water rushes out to the horizon—horses galloping in a mountain valley at night. The waves smash up the rock; I find flags of seaweed high on the worn top, forty feet up, thrown up overnight; separated water still pooled there, like the black ducks that fly desolate, forlorn, and joyful over the seething swells, who never "feel pity for themselves," and "do not lie awake weeping for their sins." In their blood cells the vultures coast with furry necks extended, watching over the desert for signs of life to end. It is not our life we need to weep for. Inside us there is some secret. We are following a narrow ledge around a mountain, we are sailing on skeletal eerie craft over the buoyant ocean.

The Starfish

It is low tide. Fog. I have climbed down the cliffs from Pierce Ranch to the tide pools. Now the ecstasy of the low tide, kneeling down, alone. In six inches of clear water I notice a purple starfish— with nineteen arms! It is a delicate purple, the color of old carbon paper, or an attic dress . . . at the webs between the arms sometimes a more intense sunset red glows through. The fingers are relaxed . . . some curled up at the tips . . . with delicate rods . . . apparently globes on top of each, as at World's Fairs, waving about. The starfish slowly moves up the groin of the rock . . . then back down . . . many of its arms rolled up now, lazily, like a puppy on its back. One arm is especially active and curved up over its own body as if a dinosaur were looking behind him.

How slowly and evenly it moves! The starfish is a glacier, going sixty miles a year! It moves over the pink rock, by means I cannot see . . . and into marvelously floating delicate brown weeds. It is about the size of the bottom of a pail. When I reach into it, it tightens and then slowly relaxes . . . I take an arm and quickly lift. The underside is a pale tan . . . Gradually, as I watch, thousands of tiny tubes begin rising from all over the underside . . . hundreds in the mouth, hundreds along the nineteen underarms . . . all looking . . . feeling . . . like a man looking for a woman . . . tiny heads blindly feeling for a rock and finding only air. A purple rim runs along the underside of every arm, with paler tubes. Probably its moving-feet.

I put him back in. He unfolds—I had forgotten how purple he was—and slides down into his rock groin, the snail-like feelers waving as if nothing had happened, and nothing has.

Driving West in 1970

My dear children, do you remember the morning
We climbed into the old Plymouth
And drove west straight toward the Pacific?

We were all the people there were.
We followed Dylan's songs all the way west.
It was Seventy; the war was over, almost;

And we were driving to the sea.
We had closed the farm, tucked in
The flap, and were eating the honey

Of distance and the word *there*.
Oh whee, we're gonna fly
Down in the easy chair. We sang that

Over and over. That's what the early
Seventies were like. We weren't afraid.
A hole had opened in the world.

We laughed at Las Vegas.
There was enough gaiety
For all of us, and ahead of us

Was the ocean. *Tomorrow's*
The day my bride's gonna come.
And the war was over, almost.

Climbing Up Mount Vision with My Little Boy

We started up. All the way he held my hand. Sometimes he falls back to bend over a banana slug, then senses how lonely the slug is, and comes running back. He never complained, and we went straight up. How much I love being with him! How much I love to feel his small leafy hand curl around my finger. He holds on, and we are flying through a cloud. On top we hunker down beneath some bushes to get out of the wind, while the girls go off to play, and he tells me the story of the little boy who wouldn't cut off his hair and give it to a witch, and so she changed him into a hollow log! A boy and girl came along, and stepped on the log—and the log said, "Oww!" They put their feet on it again, and the log said, "Oww!" Then they looked inside and saw a boy's jacket sticking out. A little boy was in there! "I can't come out, I've been changed into a hollow log." That's the end, he said.

Then I remembered a bit more—the boy and the girl went to a wise man . . . he corrected me, "It was a wise woman, Daddy," . . . and said, "How can we get him changed back into a little boy?" She said, "Here is a pearl. If a crow asks you for it, give it to him." So they went along. Pretty soon a crow came and said, "Can I have the buttons on your shirt?" The boy said, "Yes." Then the crow said, "Can I have that pearl in your shirt pocket?" "Yes." Then the crow flew up and dropped some moss down the witch's chimney. The chimney got full, the witch started to cough. The crow dropped in some more moss. Then she had to open the door, and run outside! Then the crow took an oyster, a big one, from the Johnson Oyster Company, and flew high into the air, and dropped it right on the

witch's head. And that was the end of her. And then the boy was changed back again into a little boy.

The land on top is bare, sweeping, forbidding—so unlike a little boy's mind. I asked him what he liked best about the whole walk. He said it was Bethany (an eight-year-old friend of Mary's) going pee-pee in her pants while hiding.

Welcoming a Child in the Limantour Dunes

for Micah

Thinking of a child soon to be born, I hunch down among
friendly sand grains . . . The sand grains love us, for they love
whatever lives without force, a young girl who looks out over her
life, alone, with no map, no horse, a white dress on. The sand grains
love whatever is not rushing blindly forward—I mean the mole who
is blinking at the door of his crumbly mole Vatican, and the salmon
who one morning senses in her gills the fragrant Oregon waters
crashing down. Something seems to love this planet abandoned
here at the edge of the Milky Way, and this child floating inside the
Pacific of the womb, near the walls, hearing the breakers roaring.

The Dead Seal

1.

Walking north toward the point, I come on a dead seal. From a few feet away, he looks like a brown log. The body is on its back, dead only a few hours. I stand and look at him. There's a quiver in the dead flesh: My God, he's still alive. And a shock goes through me, as if a wall of my room had fallen away.

His head is arched back, the small eyes closed; the whiskers sometimes rise and fall. He is dying. This is the oil. Here on its back is the oil that heats our houses so efficiently. Wind blows fine sand back toward the ocean. The flipper near me lies folded over the stomach, looking like an unfinished arm, lightly glazed with sand at the edges. The other flipper lies half underneath. And the seal's skin looks like an old overcoat, scratched here and there—by sharp mussel shells maybe.

I reach out and touch him. Suddenly he rears up, turns over. He gives three cries: Awaark! Awaark! Awaark!—like the cries from Christmas toys. He lunges toward me; I am terrified and leap back, though I know there can be no teeth in that jaw. He starts flopping toward the sea. But he falls over, on his face. He does not want to go back to the sea. He looks up at the sky, and he looks like an old lady who has lost her hair. He puts his chin back down on the sand, rearranges his flippers, and waits for me to go. I go.

2.

The next day I go back to say goodbye. He's dead now. But he's
not. He's a quarter mile farther up the shore. Today he is thinner,
squatting on his stomach, head out. The ribs show more: each
vertebra on the back under the coat is visible, shiny. He breathes in
and out.

A wave comes in, touches his nose. He turns and looks at
me—the eyes slanted; the crown of his head looks like a boy's
leather jacket bending over some bicycle bars. He is taking a long
time to die. The whiskers white as porcupine quills, the forehead
slopes . . . Goodbye, brother, die in the sound of the waves. Forgive
us if we have killed you. Long live your race, your inner-tube
race, so uncomfortable on land, so comfortable in the ocean.
Be comfortable in death then, when the sand will be out of your
nostrils, and you can swim in long loops through the pure death,
ducking under as assassinations break above you. You don't want to
be touched by me. I climb the cliff and go home the other way.

An Octopus

I hear a ticking on the Pacific stones. A white shape is moving in
the furry air of the seacoast. The moon narrow, the sea quiet. He
comes close; a long time the stick ticks on over the rock faces. Is
it a postal employee saddened by the sleet? It comes nearer. I talk.
The shape talks, it is a Japanese man carrying a spear and a heavy-
bellied little bag. The spear has a hook on the end. What are you
looking for, clams? No! Octopus!

Did you get any? I found three. He sits down. I get up and walk
over. May I see them? He opens the plastic bag. I turn on the
flashlight. Something wet, fantastic, womb-like, horse intestine-like.
May I take hold of one? His voice smiles. Why not? I reach in. Dry
things stick to my hands, like burrs from burdocks, compelling,
pleading, dry, poor, in debt. You boil them, then sauté them. I look
and cannot find the eyes. He is a cook. He ate them in Japan.

So the octopus is gone now from the mussel-ridden shelf with the
low roof, the pool where he waited under the thin moon, but the
sea never came back, no one came home, the door never opened.
Now he is taken away in the plastic bag, not understood, illiterate.

The Hockey Poem

for Bill Duffy

1.

The Goalie

The Boston College team has gold helmets, under which the
long black hair of the Roman centurion curls out . . . And they
begin. How weird the goalies look with their African masks! The
goalie is so lonely anyway, guarding a basket with nothing in it, his
wide lower legs wide as duck's . . . No matter what gift he is given,
he always rejects it . . . He has a number like 1, a name like Mrazek,
sometimes wobbling on his legs waiting for the puck, or curling
up like a baby in the womb to hold it, staying a second too long on
the ice.

The goalie has gone out to mid-ice, and now he sails sadly back
to his own box, slowly; he looks prehistoric with his rhinoceros legs;
he looks as if he's going to become extinct, and he's just taking
his time . . .

When the players are at the other end, he begins sadly sweeping
the ice in front of his house; he is the old witch in the woods,
waiting for the children to come home.

2.

The Attack

They all come hurrying back toward us, suddenly, knees dipping
like oil wells; they rush toward us wildly, fins waving, they are pike
swimming toward us, their gill fins expanding like the breasts of

opera singers; no, they are twelve hands practicing penmanship on the same piece of paper . . .

They flee down the court toward us like birds, swirling two and two, hawks hurrying for the mouse, hurrying down wind valleys, swirling back and forth like amoebae on the pale slide, as they sail in the absolute freedom of water and the body, untroubled by the troubled mind, only the body, with wings as if there were no grave, no gravity, only the birds sailing over the cottage far in the deep woods . . .

Now the goalie is desperate . . . he looks wildly over his left shoulder, rushing toward the other side of his cave, like a mother hawk whose chicks are being taken by two snakes . . . Suddenly he flops on the ice like a man trying to cover a whole double bed. He has the puck. He stands up, turns to his right, and drops it on the ice at the right moment; he saves it for one of his children, a mother hen picking up a seed and then dropping it . . .

But the men are all too clumsy, they can't keep track of the puck . . . no, it is the *puck*, the puck is too fast, too fast for human beings, it humiliates them constantly. The players are like country boys at the fair watching the con man— The puck always turns up under the wrong walnut shell . . .

They come down ice again, one man guiding the puck this time . . . and Ledingham comes down beautifully, like the canoe through white water, or the lover going upstream, every stroke right, like the stallion galloping up the valley surrounded by his mares and colts, how beautiful, like the body and soul crossing in a poem . . .

3.

The Fight

The player in position pauses, aims, pauses, cracks his stick
on the ice, and a cry as the puck goes in! The goalie stands up
disgusted, and throws the puck out . . .

The player with a broken stick hovers near the cage. When the
play shifts, he skates over to his locked-in teammates, who look
like a nest of bristling owls, owl babies, and they hold out a stick
to him . . .

Then the players crash together, their hockey sticks raised like
lobster claws. They fight with slow motions, as if undersea . . . they
are fighting over some woman back in the motel, but like lobsters
they forget what they're battling for; the clack of the armor plate
distracts them, and they feel a pure rage.

Or a fighter sails over to the penalty box, where ten-year-old boys
wait to sit with the criminal, who is their hero . . . They know society
is wrong, the wardens are wrong, the judges hate individuality . . .

4.

The Goalie

And this man with his peaked mask, with slits, how fantastic he
is, like a white insect who has given up on evolution in this life; his
family hopes to evolve after death, in the grave. He is ominous as a
Dark Ages knight . . . the Black Prince. His enemies defeated him in

the day, but every one of them died in their beds that night . . . At his father's funeral, he carried his own head under his arm.

He is the old woman in the shoe, whose house is never clean, no matter what she does. Perhaps this goalie is not a man at all, but a woman, all women; in her cage everything disappears in the end; we all long for it. All these movements on the ice will end, the seats will come down, the stadium walls bare . . . This goalie with his mask is a woman weeping over the children of men, that are cut down like grass, gulls that stand with cold feet on the ice . . . And at the end, she is still waiting, brushing away before the leaves, waiting for the new children developed by speed, by war . . .

Sitting on Some Rocks in Shaw Cove

I sit in a cliff hollow, surrounded by fossils and furry shells. The sea breathes and breathes under the new moon. Suddenly it rises, hurrying into the long crevices in the rock shelves, it rises like a woman's belly as if nine months has passed in a second; rising like the milk to the tiny veins, it overflows like a snake going over a low wall.

I have the sensation that half an inch under my skin there are nomad bands, stringy-legged men with fire sticks and wide-eyed babies. The rocks with their backs turned to me have something spiritual in them. On these rocks I am not afraid of death; death is like the sound of the motor in an airplane as we fly. And I still haven't found the woman I loved in some former life—how could I, when I have loved only twice on this rock, though twice in the moon, and three times in the rising water. My two daughters run toward me, laughing, arms in the air. A bird with long wings comes flying toward me in the dusk, pumping just over the darkening waves. He has flown around the whole planet; it has taken him centuries. He returns to me the lean-legged runner laughing as he runs through the stringy grasses, and gives back to me my buttons, and the soft sleeves of my sweater.

Looking at a Dead Wren in My Hand

Forgive the hours spent listening to radios, and the words of gratitude I did not say to teachers. I love your tiny rice-like legs, that are bars of music played in an empty church, and the feminine tail, where no worms of Empire have ever slept, and the intense yellow chest that makes tears come. Your tail feathers open like a picket fence, and your bill is brown, with the sorrow of a rabbi whose daughter has married an athlete. The black spot on your head is your own mourning cap.

A Hollow Tree

I bend over an old hollow cottonwood stump, still standing, waist high, and look inside. Early spring. Its Siamese temple walls are all brown and ancient. The halls have been worked on by the intricate ones. Inside the hollow walls there is privacy and secrecy, dim light. And yet some creature has died here.

On the temple floor feathers, gray feathers, many of them with a fluted white tip. Many feathers. In the silence many feathers.

August Rain

After a month and a half without rain, at last, in late August,
darkness comes at three in the afternoon, a cheerful thunder
begins, and then the rain. I set a glass out on a table to measure the
rain, and, suddenly buoyant and affectionate, go indoors to find my
children. They are upstairs, playing quietly alone in their doll-filled
rooms, hanging pictures, thoughtfully moving "the small things
that make them happy" from one side of the room to another. I
feel triumphant, without need of money, far from the grave. I walk
over the grass, watching the soaked chairs, and the cooled towels,
and sit down on my stoop, dragging a chair out with me. The rain
deepens. It rolls off the porch roof, making a great puddle near
me. The bubbles slide toward the puddle edge, become crowded,
and disappear. The black earth turns blacker, it absorbs the rain
needles without a sound. The sky is low, everything silent, as when
parents are angry . . . What has failed and been forgiven—the
leaves from last year unable to go on, lying near the foundation,
dry under the porch, retreat farther into the shadow, they give off a
faint hum, as of birds' eggs, or the tail of a dog.

The older we get the more we fail, but the more we fail the more
we feel a part of the dead straw of the universe, the corners of barns
with cow dung twenty years old, the belts left hanging over the
chairback after the bachelor has died in the ambulance on the way
to the city. These objects ride us as the child who holds on to the
dog's fur; these objects appear in our dreams; they are more and
more near us, coming in slowly from the wainscoting; they make
our trunks heavy, accumulating between trips; they lie against
the ship's side, and will nudge the hole open that lets the water in
at last.

Warning to the Reader

Sometimes farm granaries become especially beautiful when
all the oats or wheat are gone, and wind has swept the rough floor
clean. Standing inside, we see around us, coming in through the
cracks between shrunken wall boards, bands or strips of sunlight.
So in a poem about imprisonment, one sees a little light.

But how many birds have died trapped in these granaries. The
bird, seeing the bands of light, flutters up the walls and falls back
again and again. The way out is where the rats enter and leave; but
the rat's hole is low to the floor. Writers, be careful then by showing
the sunlight on the walls not to promise the anxious and panicky
blackbirds a way out!

I say to the reader, beware. Readers who love poems of light may
sit hunched in the corner with nothing in their gizzard for four
days, light failing, the eyes glazed . . . They may end as a mound of
feathers and a skull on the open boardwood floor . . .

A Chunk of Amethyst

Held up to the windowlight the amethyst has elegant corridors, that give and take light. The discipline of its many planes suggests that there is no use in trying to live forever. Its exterior is jagged, but in the inner house all is in order. Its corridors become ledges, solidified thoughts that pass each other.

This chunk of amethyst is a cool thing, hard as a dragon's tongue. The sleeping times of the whole human race lie hidden there. When the fingers fold the chunk into the palm, the palm hears organ music, the low notes that make the sins of the whole congregation resonate, and catches the criminal five miles away with a tinge of doubt.

With all its planes, it turns four or five faces toward us at once, and four or five meanings enter the mind. The exhilaration we felt as children returns . . . We feel the wind on the face as we go downhill, the sled's speed increasing . . .

SLEEPERS JOINING HANDS

1973–1986

December 23, 1926

I was born during the night-sea journey.
I love the whale with his warm organ pipes
In the mouse-killing waters, and I love the men who drift
Asleep, for three nights, in octopus waters.
Men in furs gather wood, piling the chunks by walls.
I love the snow; I need privacy as I move.
I am all alone; floating in the cooking pot
On the sea, through the night I am alone.

A Conversation

Judgment

The doctor arrives to inject the movie star against delirium tremens.
Hands that lie so often calm on the horse's mane are shaking.
His hair hangs down like a skier's hair after a fall.
From a whirlpool drops of black water fly up,
And thousands and thousands of years go by—
Like an infinite procession of walnut shells.

That hair that fell to the floor of the barbershop over thirty years
Lives on in some other place outlasting death.
And those shoelaces, shiny and twisted, that we tossed to the side,
Live on in their place, and the Hippopotamus horde arrives;
The newly dead kneel, and a tip of the lace sends them on into fire!

Affinity

I say the clumps of hair weep.
Because hair does not long for immense states;
Hair does not hate the poor.
Hair is merciful,
Like the arch of night under which the juvenile singer lolls back drunk.
Hair is excitable as a child of four or five;
It is a hammock on which the sleeper lies,
Dizzy with heat and the earth's motion.

There are golden pins lying in bureau drawers,
Whose faces shine with power. They shine
Like the cheekbones of saints radiant in their beds,
Or their great toes that light up the whole room!

Judgment

Prince Philip becomes irritable, the royal sports car
Shoots down the narrow roads;
Judy Garland is led hysterical to the Melbourne plane.
The General joins the Jehovah's Witnesses.

There are men who look, and cannot find the road,
And die coughing particles of black flesh onto neighboring roofs.

Nailheads that have been brooding on Burton's *Melancholy* under
 Baltimore rowhouses
Roll out into the street under tires,
And catch the Secretary of State
As he goes off to threaten the premiers of underdeveloped nations.

So many things are borne down by the world,
By bad luck, corpses pulled down by years of death,
Veins clogged with flakes of sludge,
Mouths from which bats escape at death,
Businessmen reborn as black whales sailing under the Arctic ice.

Affinity

I say it is all right. The earth has hair cathedrals.
The priest comes down the aisle wearing caterpillar fur.
In his sermons the toad defeats the knight.

The dying man waves his son away.
He wants his daughter-in-law to come near
So that her hair will fall over his face.

The Senator's plane falls in an orchard in Massachusetts.
And there are bitter places, knots
That leave dark pits in the sawdust . . .
The nick on the hornblade through which the mammoth escapes.

In Mourning for Betrayal

I am mourning a murder; one I have done.
I look through the window at telephone poles in water.

I reach for the notebook, and sit up in the train.
I turn on the light; I write out my vows.

The train goes on through Louisiana at night.
My breath grows slow and heavy, in the melancholy.

The betrayer left the garden in the early spring night.
He fed on his own pity, and grew fat on that.

Orrin and his wife, asleep on bare mattresses,
Woke; I dream I put my head down between them and wept.

Pulling up from far below, the water is born,
Spreading white tomb-clothes on the rocky shore.

Chinese Tomb Guardians

Oh yes, I love you, book of my confessions,
Where what was swallowed, pushed away, sunken,
Driven down, begins to rise from the earth
Once more, and the madness and rage from the wells.
The buried is still buried, like cows who eat
In a collapsed strawpile all winter to get out.

Something inside me is still imprisoned in winter straw,
Or far back in the mountain where Charlemagne sleeps,
Or under the water, hard to get to, guarded by women.
Enough rises from that place to darken my poems;
Perhaps too much; and what remains down there
Makes a faint glow in the dead leaves.

I am less than half risen. I see how carefully
I have covered my tracks as I wrote,
How well I have brushed over the past with my tail.
Faces look at me from the shallow waters,
Where I have pushed them down—
Father and mother pushed into the dark.

What am I in my ambition and loneliness?
I am the dust that fills the cracks on the ocean floor.
Floating like the stingray, used to the weight
Of the ocean floor, retreating to a cave,
I live as a lizard or a winged shark,
Darting out at times to wound others, or get food.

How do we know that the hidden will ever rise?
How do we know that the buried will be revealed?
Some beings get used to life underneath.
Some dreams do not want to move into the light.
Some want to, but they can't; they can't make their way out,
Because someone is guarding the posts of the door.

Have you seen those Chinese tomb guardians
Left at the closed door? They stand with one knee raised;
They half-stand, half-dance, half-rage, half-shout—
Hot-tempered muscle-bulgers, big-kneed brow-bulgers.
They scowl for eternity at the half-risen.
What do you have that can get past them?

LOVING A WOMAN IN TWO WORLDS

1978–1985

and Related Poems

The Third Body

A man and a woman sit near each other, and they do not long
At this moment to be older, or younger, or born
In any other nation, or any other time, or any other place.
They are content to be where they are, talking or not-talking.
Their breaths together feed someone whom we do not know.
The man sees the way his fingers move;
He sees her hands close around a book she hands to him.
They obey a third body that they share in common.
They have promised to love that body.
Age may come; parting may come; death will come!
A man and a woman sit near each other;
As they breathe they feed someone we do not know,
Someone we know of, whom we have never seen.

The Horses at the Tank

Every breath taken in by the man
Who loves, and the woman who loves,
Goes to fill the water tank
Where the spirit horses drink.

The Whole Moisty Night

The Viking ship sails into the full harbor.
The body meets its wife far out at sea.
Its lamp remains lit the whole moisty night.
Water pours down, faint flute notes in the sound of the water.

Night Frogs

I wake and find myself in the woods, far from the castle.
The train hurtles through lonely Louisiana at night.
The sleeper turns to the wall; delicate
Aircraft dive toward earth.

A woman whispers to me, urges me to speak truths.
"I am afraid you won't be honest with me."
More than half of the moon rolls on in shadow.
Loons wheel cries through lower waters.

Some invisible being with hooves tramples
The grasses while the horses are asleep.
Something flat slips under the door
And lies exhausted on the floor in the morning.

I threw some parts of me away at ten,
Others at twenty, a lot around twenty-eight.
I wanted to thin myself out as a wire is thinned.
Is there enough left of me now to be honest?

The lizard moves stiffly over November roads.
How much I am drawn toward my parents! I walk back
And forth, looking toward the old landing.
Night frogs give out the croak of the planet turning.

Winter Poem

The quivering wings of the winter ant
Wait for lean winter to end.
I love you in slow, dim-witted ways,
Hardly speaking, one or two words only.

What caused us each to live hidden?
A wound, the wind, a word, a parent.
Sometimes we wait in a helpless way,
Awkwardly, not whole and not healed.

When we hid the wound, we fell back
From a human to a shelled life.
Now we feel the ant's hard chest,
The carapace, the silent tongue.

This must be the way of the ant,
The winter ant, the way of those
Who are wounded and want to live:
To breathe, to sense another, and to wait.

At Midocean

All day I loved you in a fever, holding on to the tail of the horse.
I overflowed whenever I reached out to touch you.
My hand moved over your body, covered
With its dress,
Burning, rough, the hand of an animal's foot moving over leaves.
The rainstorm retires, clouds open, sunlight
Sliding over ocean water a thousand miles from land.

Listening to the Köln Concert

After we had loved each other intently,
We heard notes tumbling together,
In late winter, and we heard ice
Falling from the ends of twigs.

The notes abandon so much as they move.
They are the food not eaten, the comfort
Not taken, the lies not spoken.
The music is my attention to you.

And when the music came again,
Later in the day, I saw tears in your eyes.
I saw you turn your face away
So that others would not see.

When men and women come together,
How much they have to abandon! Wrens
Make their nests of fancy threads
And string ends, animals

Abandon all their money each year.
What is that men and women leave?
Harder than wren's doing, they have
To abandon their longing for the perfect.

The inner nest not made by instinct
Will never be quite round,
And each has to enter the nest
Made by the other imperfect bird.

Love Poem in Twos and Threes

What kind of people
Are these? Some stammer
Of land, some
Want nothing but light—
No house or land
Thrown away for a woman,
No ample recklessness.
How much I need
A woman's soul, felt
In my own knees,
Shoulders and hands.
I was born sad!
I am a northern goat
Of winter light,
Up to my knees in snow.
Standing by you, I am
Glad as the clams
At high tide, eerily
Content as the amorous
Ocean owls.

Poem on Sleep

"Then the bright being disguised as a seal dove into the deep billows."
I go on loving you after we are asleep.
I know the ledges where we sit all night looking out over the briny sea,
And the open places where we coast in sleekness through the sea.

And where is the hunter who is cunning? The practical part of me?
Oh he is long since gone, dispersed among the bold grasses.
The one he does not know of remains afloat and awake all night;
That one lies on luminous boulders, dives, his coat sleek, his eyes open.

The Horse of Desire

"Yesterday I saw a face
That gave off light."
I wrote that the first time
I saw you; now the lines
Written that morning
Are twenty years old.
What is it that
We see and don't see?

When a horse swings
His head, how easily
His shoulders follow.
When the right thing happens,
The whole body knows.
The road covered with stones
Turns to a soft river
Moving among reeds.

I love you in those reeds,
And in the bass
Quickening there.
My love is in the demons
Gobbling the waters,
My desire in their swollen
Foreheads poking
Earthward out of the trees.

The bear between my legs
Has one eye only,
Which he offers
To God to see with.
The two beings below with no
Eyes at all love you
With the slow persistent
Intensity of the blind.

Conversation with a Holy Woman Not Seen for Many Years

After so many years, I come walking to you.
You say: "You have come after so long?"
I could not come earlier. My shabby mouth,
With its cavernous thirst, ate the seeds of longing
That should have been planted. Awkward and baffled,
Dishonest, I slept. And I dreamt of sand.
Your eyes in sorrow do not laugh.
I say, "I have come after so many years."

Two Middle-Aged Lovers

An Etching by Dürer

The man and the woman linger under a tree,
Soberly, standing near his horse.
Man and woman hear the low muttering speech
Instinct makes to instinct.
Their canoe shoots down the narrow channel;
The climber goes rock by rock up the mountainside.
The yaks, hair blowing, disappear into the storm.

In Rainy September

In rainy September, when leaves grow down into the dark,
I put my forehead down to the damp, seaweed-smelling sand.
The time has come. I have put off choosing for years,
Perhaps whole lives. The fern has no choice but to live;
For this crime it receives earth, water, and night.

We close the door. "I have no claim on you." Dusk
Comes. You say, "The love I had with you is enough."
We know we could live apart from one another.
The sheldrake floats apart from the flock.
The oak tree puts out leaves alone on the lonely hillside.

Men and women before us have accomplished this.
I would see you, and you me, once a year.
We would be two kernels, and not be planted.
We stay in the room, door closed, lights out.
I weep with you without shame and without honor.

The Indigo Bunting

I go to the door often.
Night and summer. Crickets
Lift their cries.
I know you are out.
You are driving
Late through the summer night.

I do not know what will happen.
I have no claim on you.
I am one star
You have as guide; others
Love you, the night
So dark over the Azores.

You have been working outdoors,
Gone all week. I feel you
In this lamp lit
So late. As I reach for it
I feel myself
Driving through the night.

I love a firmness in you
That disdains the trivial
And regains the difficult.
You become part then
Of the firmness of night,
The granite holding up walls.

There were women in Egypt who
Supported with their firmness the stars
As they revolved,
Hardly aware
Of the passage from night
To day and back to night.

I love you where you go
Through the night, not swerving,
Clear as the indigo
Bunting in her flight,
Passing over two
Thousand miles of ocean.

In the Time of Peony Blossoming

When I come near the red peony flower
I tremble as water does near thunder,
As the well does when the plates of earth move,
Or the tree when fifty birds leave at once.

The peony says that we have been given a gift,
And it is not the gift of this world.
Behind the leaves of the peony
There is a world still darker, that feeds many.

The Moose

The Arctic moose drinks at the tundra's edge,
Swirling the watercress with his mouth.
How fresh the water is, the coolness of the far North.
A light wind moves through the deep firs.

The Ram

The ram walks over the minty grass.
The hawk ruffles his shoulder feathers.
Two chooks sit with feathers overlapping.
Just before dark big snowflakes fall.

The Heron Drinking

The bird dips to take some water in its bill.
We receive what the nation cannot give.
We are thirsty for the heron
And the lake, the touch of the bill on the water.

In the Month of May

In the month of May, when all leaves open,
I see when I walk how well all things
Lean on each other, how the bees work,
The fish make their living the first day.
Monarchs fly high; then I understand
I love you with what in me is unfinished.

I love you with what in me is still
Changing, what has no head or arms
Or legs, what has not found its body.
And why shouldn't the miraculous,
Caught on this earth, visit
The old man alone in his hut?

And why shouldn't Gabriel, who loves honey,
Be fed with our own radishes and walnuts?
And lovers, tough ones, how many there are
Whose holy bodies are not yet born.
Along the roads, I see so many places
I would like us to spend the night.

A Dream of an Afternoon with a Woman
I Did Not Know

I woke up, and went out. Not yet dawn.
A rooster claimed he was the sickle moon.
The windmill was a ladder that ended at a gray cloud.
A feed grinder was growling at a nearby farm.

Frost has made clouds of the weeds overnight.
In my dream we stopped for coffee. We sat alone
Near a fireplace, near delicate cups.
I loved that afternoon, and the rest of my life.

A Man and a Woman and a Blackbird

> A man and a woman
> are one.
> A man and a woman and a blackbird
> are one.
> —Wallace Stevens

When the two rivers
Join in the cloudy chamber,
So many alien nights
In our twenties, alone
On interior mountains,
Forgotten. Blackbirds
Walk around our feet
As if they shared
In what we know.
We know and we don't know
What the heron feels
With his wing-
Tip feathers stretched
Out in the air above
The flooded lake,
Or the delicious constellations
The pig sees
Past his wild snout.
A man and a woman
Sit near each other. On
The windowplace
Ice.
The man says: "How
Is it
I have never loved
Ice before?
If I have not loved ice,
What have I loved?
Loved the dead

In their Sumerian
Fish-cloaks?
The vultures celebrating?
The soldiers
And the poor?"
And yet
For one or two
Moments,
In our shared grief
And exile,
We hang our harps
On the willows,
And the willows
Join us,
And the man
And the woman
And the blackbird are one.

The Ant on the Board

It is not only the ant that walks on the carpenter's board alone,
Nor the March turtle on his boulder surrounded by March water . . .
I know there are whitecaps that are born and die alone.
There is a rocky pasture, and a new one nearby, with a path between.

I know there are branchy stalks, dropped to the ground last summer,
And tires, half worn-down, lifted to the gas-station owner's rack.
All of them I saw today, and all of them were dear to me,
And the rough-barked young cottonwood alone on the windy shore.

What we exerience is not the ant on the carpenter's board
Only, nor the March turtle on his wet boulder,
Nor the rising whirlwind, nor the certainty, nor the steady gaze,
Nor the meeting by the altar, nor the rising sun only.

A Love That I Have in Secret

Who is this in me who loves you so?
It must be four fiery men;
They make up a man who loves you.
His grief and his music cannot
Be explained: it is wound inside
An ocean shell, held up to the ears
Of old Egyptian ladies soon be born.

Do these speculations confuse adultery
With light and make lies sound civilized?
Say then that it is a Northern love,
A barbarous and shadowy thing,
A turbid river where the moose drinks,
His antlers lift as my body lifts
When we make love upon the waters.

Come Live with Me

Driving among the moraine hills
Near Battle Lake, around Vining,
I admire the hand-cut fenceposts,
The orchards, the hay stored for winter.

I want you to come with me and see
The cowtracks winding down the hills,
The chunks of oak piled for winter,
The small lakes folded in and gleaming.

An Evening When the Full Moon Rose
as the Sun Set

The sun goes down in the dusty April night.
"You know it could be alive!"
The sun is round, massive, compelling, sober, on fire.
It moves swiftly through the tree stalks of the Lundin grove as we
 drive past . . .
The legs of a bronze god walking at the edge of the world, unseen
 by many,
On his archaic errands, doubled up on his own energy.
He guides his life by his dreams,
When we look again he is gone.

Turning toward Milan, we see the other one, the moon, whole and rising.
Three wild geese make dark spots in that part of the sky.
Under the shining one the pastures leap forward,
Grass fields rolling as in October, the sow-colored fields near the river.
The rising one lights the pair of pintails alert in the shallow pond.
It shines on those faithful to each other, alert in the early night,
And the life of faithfulness goes by like a river,
With no one noticing it.

THIS BODY IS MADE OF CAMPHOR AND GOPHERWOOD

1973–1980

Walking Swiftly

When I wake, I hear sheep eating apple peels just outside the screen. The trees are heavy, soaked, cold and hushed, the sun just rising. All seems calm, and yet somewhere inside I am not calm. We live in wooden buildings made of two-by-fours, making the landscape nervous for a hundred miles. And the Emperor when he was sixty called for rhinoceros horn, for sky-blue phoenix eggs shaped from veined rock, dipped in rooster blood. Around him the wasps kept guard, the hens continued their patrol, the oysters open and close all questions. The heat inside the human body grows, it does not know where to throw itself—for a while it knots into will, heavy, burning, sweet, then into generosity, that longs to take on the burdens of others, and then into mad love. The artist walks swiftly to his studio, and carves oceanic waves into the dragon's mane.

Wings Folding Up

The cucumbers are thirsty, their big leaves turn away from the wind. I water them after supper; the hose lies curled near the rhubarb. The wind sound blows through the head; a smile appears on the sitter's face as he sits down under a tree. What can be comforted in us words help, the sunken islands speak to us . . .

Is this world animal or vegetable? Others love us, the cabbages love the earth, the earth is fond of the heavens—a new age comes close through the dark, an elephant's trunk waves in the darkness, so much is passing away, so many disciplines already gone, but the energy in the double flower does not falter, the wings fold up around the sitting man's face. And these cucumber leaves are my body, and my thighs, and toes stretched out in the wind . . . Well, waterer, how will you get through this night without water?

Going Out to Check the Ewes

My friend, this body is food for the thousand dragons of the air, each dragon light as a needle. This body loves us, and carries us home from our hoeing.

It is ancient, and full of the bales of sleep. In its vibrations the sun rolls along under the earth; the spouts over the ocean curl into our stomach. Water revolves, making spouts seen by skull eyes at mid-ocean. This body of herbs and gopherwood, this blessing, this is a lone ridge patrolled by water . . . I get up, morning is here. The stars are still out; the black winter sky looms over the unborn lambs. The barn is cold before dawn, the gates slow.

This body longs for itself far out at sea, it floats in the black heavens, it is a brilliant being, locked in the prison of human dullness . . .

We Love This Body

My friend, this body is made of energy compacted and whirling.
It is the wind that carries the henhouse down the road dancing,
and an instant later lifts all four walls apart. It is the horny
thumbnail of the retired railway baron, over which his children
skate on Sunday, it is the forehead bone that does not rot, the
woman priest's hair still fresh among Shang ritual things . . .

We love this body as we love the day we first met the person who
led us away from this world, as we love the gift we gave one morning
on impulse, in a fraction of a second, that we still see every day, as
we love the human face, fresh after lovemaking, more full of joy
than a wagonload of hay.

Finding the Father

This body offers to carry us for nothing—as the ocean carries logs—so on some days the body wails with its great energy, it smashes up the boulders, lifting small crabs, that flow around the sides. Someone knocks on the door, we do not have time to dress. He wants us to come with him through the blowing and rainy streets, to the dark house. We will go there, the body says, and there find the father whom we have never met, who wandered in a snowstorm the night we were born, who then lost his memory, and has lived since longing for his child, whom he saw only once . . . while he worked as a shoemaker, as a cattle herder in Australia, as a restaurant cook who painted at night. When you light the lamp you will see him. He sits there behind the door . . . the eyebrows so heavy, the forehead so light . . . lonely in his whole body, waiting for you.

The Cry Going Out Over Pastures

I love you so much with this curiously alive and lonely body. My body is a young hawk sitting on a tree by the Mississippi, in early spring, before any green has appeared on the earth beneath. Some days walnut hollows in my chest fill with crackling light and shadows. There birds drink from water drops . . . My body loves you with what it extracts from the prudent man, hunched over his colony of lizards; and with that it loves you madly, beyond all rules and conventions. Even the six holes in the flute move about under the dark man's fingers, and the piercing cry goes out over the grown-up pastures no one sees or visits at dusk except the deer, out of all enclosures, who has never seen any bed but his own of wild grass.

I first met you when I had been alone for nine days, and now my lonely hawk body longs to be with you, whom it remembers . . . it knew how close we are, we would always be. There is death but also this closeness, this joy when the bee rises into the air above his hive to find the sun, to become the son, and the traveler moves through exile and loss, through murkiness and failure, to touch the earth again of his own kingdom and kiss the ground . . .

What shall I say of this? I say, praise to the first man who wrote down this joy clearly, for we cannot remain in love with what we cannot name . . .

The Owlets at Nightfall

The sun is sinking. Each minute the air darker. The night thickens near the ground, pulls my body down to it. And if my body is earth, then what? Then I am down here, thickening as night comes on.

There are earth things, earthly, joined, they are snuggled down in one manger, one sweep of arms holds them, one clump of pine, the owlets sit together in one hollow tree . . .

When night comes what has been sun in me all day will drop underneath the earth, and travel sizzling along the underneath-ocean-darkness path . . . There a hundred developed saints lie stretched out, throwing bits of darkness onto the road.

At midnight what has been moon in me will also vanish. I will go down toward utter darkness and find myself in the prison cell with Joseph.

The Lover's Body as a Community of Protozoa

This body is made of bone and excited protozoa . . . and it is
with my body that I love the fields. How do I know what I feel but
what the body tells me? Erasmus thinking in the snow, translators
of Virgil who burn up the whole room, the man in furs reading the
Arabic astrologer falls off his three-legged stool in astonishment—
this is the body, so beautifully carved inside, with the curves of the
inner ear, and the husk so rough, knuckle-brown.

As we walk we enter the magnetic fields of other bodies, and
every smell we take in the communities of protozoa see; and a
being inside leaps up toward it, as a horse rears at the starting gate.
When you and I come near each other, we are drawn down into the
sweetest pools of slowly circling energies, slowly circling smells.

Each living thing throws itself down before the dawn,
And the night opens itself out behind it,
And inside its own center it lives!

So the space between two people diminishes; it grows less and
less; no one to weep; they merge at last. The sound that pours from
the fingertips awakens clouds of cells far inside the other's body,
and beings unknown to us start out in a pilgrimage to their Saviour,
to their holy place. Their holy place is a small black stone, that they
remember from Protozoic times, when it was rolled away from a door.

The clouds of cells awaken, intensify, swarm; and they dance
inside a ray of sunlight so thin we cannot even see it. But to them,
each ray is a vast palace with thousands of rooms. From the cells,
praise sentences begin to the rise to the man and women singing in
the room. A voice says: "Now do you still remain ungrateful? Do you
still say there is no road?"

for Lewis Thomas and his The Lives of a Cell

Blessings on the Dweller

There is a dweller in the dark cabin.
Who is this, someone hearing and telling?
The relative has come, the dark ocean shell.
There is something solid, a dweller in the dark cabin.

The face of the cabin awakens—
What the savage loves in his madness.
The cavern itself wakes up. There is a traveler—
He has to be awake—sleeping in the cabin.

Far down in my dream, I dreamt a bearded fish,
An old one, immense, slipped into my arms.
The traveler gone so long has returned.
There is a dweller in the dark cabin.

The linen merchants find Joseph singing.
Tiny bits of thread join into longer strings,
Indistinguishable from music when they join,
Something mingling, continual, eternal.

Who is that? A man travels here and there,
Something slowly gains solidity in November air.
Our relative from the lair and the shell has come.
There is a dweller in the dark cabin.

THE MAN IN THE BLACK COAT TURNS

1980–1984

Snowbanks North of the House

Those great sweeps of snow that stop suddenly six feet from the house . . .
Thoughts that go so far.
The boy gets out of high school and reads no more books;
The son stops calling home.
The mother puts down her rolling pin and makes no more bread.
And the wife looks at her husband one night at a party, and loves
 him no more.
The energy leaves the wine, and the minister falls leaving the church.
It will not come closer—
The one inside moves back, and the hands touch nothing, and are safe.

The father grieves for his son, and will not leave the room where the
 coffin stands.
He turns away from his wife, and she sleeps alone.

And the sea lifts and falls all night, the moon goes on through the
 unattached heavens alone.
The toe of the shoe pivots
In the dust . . .
And the man in the black coat turns, and goes back down the hill.
No one knows why he came, or why he turned away, and did not
 climb the hill.

The Sense of Decline

The Farallones seals clubbed,
Whales gone, tortoises
Taken from islands
To fill the holds; the Empire

Dying in its provincial cities.
No one to repair the baths;
Farms turned over
To soldiers; the judges corrupt.

The wagon behind bounces,
Breaking on boulders, back
And forth, slowly
Smashed to pieces. This crumb-

Ling darkness is a reality
Too, the feather
On the snow, the rooster's
Half-eaten body nearby.

And other worlds I do not see:
The Old People's Home
At dusk, the slow
Murmur of conversation.

Visiting Emily Dickinson's Grave
with Robert Francis

A black iron fence closes the graves in, its ovals delicate as wine stems. They resemble those chapel windows on the main Aran island, made narrow in the fourth century so that not too much rain would drive in . . . It is April, clear and dry. Curls of grass rise around the nearby gravestones.

The Dickinson house is not far off. She arrived here one day, at fifty-six, Robert says, carried over the lots between by six Irish laboring men, when her brother refused to trust her body to a carriage. The coffin was darkened with violets and pine boughs, as she covered the immense distance between the solid Dickinson house and this plot . . .

The distance *is* immense, the distances through which Satan and his helpers rose and fell, oh vast areas, the distances between stars, between the first time love is felt in the sleeves of the dress, and the death of the person who was in that room . . .

Exultation is the going
Of the inland soul to sea,
Past the houses, past the headlands
Into deep Eternity.

. . . the distance between the feet and head as you lie down, the distance between the mother and father, through which we pass reluctantly.

About her parents and their habit of prayer, Emily wrote to a friend, "My family addresses an Eclipse every morning, which they call their 'Father.'"

As we leave the cemetery, Robert says, "My apartment is small, but I took it because I could see her grave from my window." He has given his life to seeing what is far away. He used to serve a visitor— in a small glass—wine made from his own dandelions. "Can you mistake us? . . . For this I have abandoned all my other lives."

Mourning Pablo Neruda

Water is practical,
Especially in
August.
Faucet water
That drops
Into the buckets
I carry
To the young
Willow trees
Whose leaves have been eaten
Off by grasshoppers.
Or this jar of water
That lies next to me
On the car seat
As I drive to my shack.
When I look down,
The seat all
Around the jar
Is dark,
For water doesn't intend
To give, it gives
Anyway,
And the jar of water
Lies
There quivering
As I drive
Through a countryside
Of granite quarries,
Stones

Soon to be shaped
Into blocks for the dead,
The only
Thing they have
Left that is theirs.

For the dead remain inside
Us, as water
Remains
Inside granite—
Hardly at all—
For their job is to
Go
Away,
And not come back,
Even when we ask them,
But water
Comes to us—
It doesn't care
About us, it goes
Around us, on the way
To the Minnesota River,
To the Mississippi River,
To the Gulf,
Always closer
To where
It has to be.
No one lays flowers
On the grave

Of water,
For it is not
Here,
It is
Gone.

Fifty Men Sitting Together

1.

After a long walk in the woods clear cut for lumber,
Lit up by only a few young pines,
I turn home,
Drawn to water. A band of shadow
Softens half the lake,
Draws the shadow
Down from westward hills.
I see in that massive
Masculine shadow
Fifty men sitting together
In hall or crowded room,
Lifting something indistinct
Up into the resonating night.

2.

Near shore, reeds stand about in groups
Unevenly as if they might
Finally ascend
To the sky all together!
Each reed has its own
Thin thread
Of darkness inside so
It is relaxed
And rooted in the mud.
So the son who has lived

Protected by the mother lives protected
By reeds in the joy of the half darkness.

3.

The woman stays in the kitchen, and does not want
To waste fuel by lighting a lamp,
As she waits
For the drunk husband to come home.
Then she serves him
Food in silence.
What does the son do?
He cleaves to her,
Looks down,
Goes outdoors to feed with wild
Things, lives in the reeds,
Pulls away from men,
Reaches upward, looks to the sky, ascends.

4.

How far he is from working men when he is forty!
From all men! The men singing
Chant far out
On the water grounded in downward shadow.
He cannot go there because
He still hopes

He will not die. He will
Not throw
Himself into the shadow.
The dark comes down slowly,
The way snow falls,
Or herds pass a cave mouth
I look up at the other shore; it is night.

The Prodigal Son

The Prodigal Son is kneeling in the husks.
My friend, the steering column in his chest,
Cried: "Don't let me die, doctor!"
The swine go on feeding in the sunlight.

When he folds his hands, his knees
On corncobs, he sees the smoke of ships
Floating off the isles of Tyre and Sidon,
And father beyond father beyond father.

An old man once being dragged across
The floor by his shouting son, cried:
"Don't drag me any farther than that crack on the floor—
I only dragged my father that far!"

So this dragging of father and son goes on
Century after century after century.
There are brothers, some favorites, some
Not. Neither brother gets what he wants.

My father is seventy-five years old.
Looking at his face, I look into water.
How difficult it is! Under the water
There's a door that the pigs have gone through.

Eleven O'Clock at Night

I lie alone in my bed; cooking and stories are over at last, and some peace comes. And what did I do today? I wrote down some thoughts on sacrifice that other people had, but couldn't relate them to my own life. I brought my daughter to the bus—on the way to Minneapolis for a haircut—and I waited twenty minutes with her in the somnolent hotel lobby. I wanted the mail to bring some praise for my ego to eat, and was disappointed. I added up my bank balance, and found only sixty-five dollars, when I need over a thousand to pay the bills for this month alone. So this is how my life is passing before the grave?

The walnut of my brain glows. I feel it irradiate the skull. I am aware of the consciousness I have, and I mourn the consciousness I do not have.

Stubborn things lie and stand around me—the walls, a bookcase with its few books, the footboard of the bed, my shoes that lie against the blanket tentatively, as if they were animals sitting at table, my stomach with its curved demand. I see the bedside lamp, and the thumb of my right hand, the pen my fingers hold so trustingly. There is no way to escape from these. Many times in poems I have escaped—from myself. I sit for hours and at last see a pinhole in the top of the pumpkin, and I slip out that pinhole, gone! The genie expands and is gone; no one can get him back in the bottle again; he is hovering over a car cemetery somewhere.

Now more and more I long for what I cannot escape from. The sun shines on the side of the house across the street. Eternity is near, but it is not *here*. My shoes, my thumbs, my stomach, remain inside the room, and for that there is no solution. Consciousness comes so slowly, half our life passes, we eat and talk asleep—and for that there is no solution. Since Pythagoras died the world has

gone down a certain path, and I cannot change that. Someone not in my family invented the microscope, and Western eyes grew the intense will to pierce down through its darkening tunnel. Air itself is willing without pay to lift the 707's wing, and for that there is no solution. Pistons and rings have appeared in the world; valves usher gas vapor in and out of the theater box ten times a second; and for that there is no solution. Something besides my will loves the woman I love. I love my children, though I did not know them before they came. I change every day. For the winter dark of late December there is no solution.

Kennedy's Inauguration

Sister de Chantal hands
Me the sticky pod
Of the Sweet Gum Tree.
New to me, it's the size
Of a cow's eyeball, brown
And prickly. Its seeing
Is all gone, finished,
Exploded out
Through the eyeholes.
I turn it in my palm;
It pricks the tender skin.

The hard-edged eye-
Holes resemble hen
Beaks widening in fear.
Are the dogs coming?
Where an ear
Should be, another
Beak is opening, where
A comb should be, another
Beak is opening. Fear
Of the dogs makes
The cries more hoarse.

And what did I do today?
I drove the long way twice
So as not to pass
The funeral home.

I had three conversations,
All distant. If I know
So well how to live,
Then why am I frightened?
A man's head has been
Broken by a cannonball,
One eye dangles out.

King Leopold's men
Set up rubber plantations,
Bring Bantus in
To bleed the trees. Some
Skip work. "If he's
A father, the best thing
Is to cut off the hands."
A photographer catches
The scene: The son's hands
Lie on the ground
Between the father's feet.

In Nineteen Thirty-eight,
The Brownshirts arrive,
Take women away
Into breeding hotels.
Jews and Gypsies
Bleed the trees.
It is all prepared.
Marilyn Monroe is there.

I see her drugged
Arm hanging out
Over the side of the bed.

Out of her back comes the Marine's
Cry for the medic.
His foot is lying a few
Feet away. His
Lips are open, the brain
Is missing—only
The throat and the cry are there.
And the President
In the cold, the back of his head
Still intact, lays
One hand on the Bible.

Words Rising

I open my journal, write a few
Sounds with green ink, and suddenly
Fierceness enters me, stars
Begin to revolve, and pick up
Alligator dust from under the ocean.
Writing and writing, I feel the bushy
Tail of the Great Bear
Reach down and brush the seafloor.

All those deaths we lived in the sunlit
Shelves of the Dordogne, the tunes we sang
To the newborn and the skeletons
Of Papua, those murderous moments
We died—wounded—under the cloak
Of an animal's sniffing, all those lives
Return, and the grassy nights
We ran in the moonlight for hours.

These deaths and lives return through
Language. When we feed a few words
With private grief, the shame
We knew before we could
Invent the wheel, they come.
The old earth-fragrance remains
In the word *and*. We experience
The in its lonely suffering.

We are bees then; honey is our language.
Now the honey lies stored in caves

Beneath us, and the sound of words
Sometimes carries what we do not.
We see a million hands with dusty
Palms turned up inside the verb
To feed. And there are eternal vows
Held inside the word *Jericho.*

Blessings then on the man who labors
In his room writing stanzas on the lamb.
And blessings on the woman who picks the brown
Seeds of solitude in afternoon light
Out of the black seeds of loneliness.
Blessings on the dictionary maker, huddled
Among his bearded words and on the setter of songs
Who sleeps at night inside his violin case.

MEDITATIONS ON THE INSATIABLE SOUL

1990–1994

Time Runs Backward After Death

1.

Samson, grinding bread for widows and orphans,
Forgets he is wronged, and the answers
The Philistines wrangled out of him go back
Into the lion. The bitter and the sweet marry.
He himself wronged the lion. Now the wheat
Caresses the wind with its wifely tail; the donkey
Runs in the long grass; and having glimpsed heaven,
The fox's body saunters the tawny earth.

2.

After death the soul returns to drinking milk
And honey in its sparse home. Broken lintels
Rejoin the sunrise gates, and bees sing
In the sour meat. Once more in the cradle his
Hair grows long and golden; Delilah's scissors
Turn back into two tiny and playful swords.
Samson, no longer haunted by sunset and shadows,
Sinks down in the Eastern ocean and is born.

Visiting My Father

1.

Your chest, hospital gown
Awry, looks
Girlish today.
It is your bluish
Reptile neck
That has known weather.
I said to you, "Are
You ready to die?"
"I am," you said,
"It's too boring
Around here." He has in mind
Some other place
Less boring. "He's
Not ready to go,"
The doctor said.
There must have been
A fire that nearly
Blew out, or a large
Soul, inadequately
Feathered, that became
Cold and angered.
Some four-year-old boy
In you, chilled by your
Mother, misprized
By your father, said,
"I will defy, I will
Win anyway, I

Will show *them*."
When Alice's well-
Off sister offered to
Take your two boys
During the Depression,
You said it again.
Now you bring that
Defiant mood to death.
The four-year-old
Old man in you does as
He likes: he likes
To stay alive.
Through him you
Get revenge,
Persist, endure,
Overlive, overwhelm,
Get on top.
You gave me
This, and I do
Not refuse it.
It is
In me.

2.

My Father at Eighty-six

You are eighty-
Six, and while we
Talk suddenly
Fall asleep.
Would you have been
Proud of me
If I had lived
More like you?
In this same hospital
Room, drying out
Thirty-five years
Ago, you said to me:
"Are you happy?"
I was twenty-eight.
"Happiness is not one
Of the aims I have
Set for my life."
You were alarmed.
I was bluffing, as
Isolated as you.
Now you have almost
Reached the last station.
Shall I say that you
Misspent your life?
You stood vibrating

On a threshing machine,
Pulleys, choppers, shakers
Beneath you,
And kept your balance
Mostly.
I walked on a rope,
Carrying six
Children on my shoulders,
Felt their love.
A woman had
A message for me
And it arrived.
Now for the first time
I can see your skull
Below your closed
Grape-like eyes.
Some modest,
Luminous
Thing has happened.
Is that all?
What did we expect?

3.

The Hard Breathing

Your hard breathing
We all three
Notice. To continue
To live here,
One must take air.
But taking air
Commits you
To sharing it
With the puma and the eagle.
When breathing stops
You will be free
Of that company.
You came from the water
World, and do not
Want to change
Again. My mother
Does not remember
The water world.
Nieces are here
In this world, nephews,
Classmates, a son.
You sit with puzzled eyes
Now, as if to say,
"Where is that
Reckless man

Who laughed and
Made me laugh?
Is it this man
With gaunt cheeks
On the bed?
All those times
I drove into town,
Carefully, over
Packed snow, is this
What it comes to?" Yes,
Yes it is, my
Dear mother.
The tablecloths
You saved are all
Gone; the baked
Corn dish you
Made for your boys,
The Christmas Eves,
Opening perfume—
Evening in Paris—
From your husband,
The hope that a man
Would alter his
Habits for you—
They are all gone.
The nurse takes my father
For his bath.
You and I wait
Wait here for Jacob

To come back.
"What sort of
Flowers are those?"
"Daisies," I say.
A few minutes later,
You ask again.
What can I do but
Feel the invisible
River go through
Me, and sit
Here with you?

4.

Something Has Come

My mother and I sit
In the hospital room.
What can we say
To each other?
That we are nothing
When the Man
Leaves the room?
That we are bound
By our breathing
To this troubled place?
That I am a son
And you are a mother,
And that something
Has come
Between us,
So that we forget
What has saved us.

5.

The Komodo Dragon

My father and I
Swim a half mile
Or so apart
In a cold sea.
Each of us senses
The other's strokes,
But we swim far from
The care of women.
I swim on, asking
My shoulders why
My lower half
Feels so heavy.
Only my arms
Lift, the ocean
Pulls the rest
Of me down.
I know that far
Below us, scattered
On the ocean floor,
There are Model A
Engines, spoked wheels
From horse rakes,
Engine blocks
Broken apart,
Snapped plow-

Shares, drive shafts
Sticking from sand,
Useless cutter-bars.
Our failures have
Solidified there,
Rusting
In saline water.
We worked all day
Through till mid-
Night and couldn't
Keep the swather
Going, nothing helps,
Drove a piston
Right through the block.
It won't do.
And behind us
A large beast
Swims—four or
Five miles back,
Spines on his nose,
Fins like the
Komodo dragon,
Spiny whiskers,
Following us.

6.

The Pharaoh's Servant

My father's large ears
Hear everything.
A hermit wakes
And sleeps in a hut
Underneath
His gaunt cheeks.
His eyes blue, alert,
Disappointed,
And suspicious,
Complain
I do not bring him
The same sort of
Jokes the nurses
Do. He is a bird
Waiting to be fed—
Mostly beak—an eagle
Or a vulture,
Or the Pharaoh's servant
Just before death.
My arm on the bedrail
Rests there, relaxed,
With new love. All
I know of the Troubadours
I bring to this bed.
I do not want

Or need to be shamed
By him any longer.
The general of shame
Has discharged
Him, and left him
In this small provincial
Egyptian town.
If I do not wish
To shame him, then
Why not love him?
His long hands,
Large, veined,
Capable, can still
Retain hold of what
He wanted:
Six farms. But
Is that what he
Desired? Some
Powerful engine
Of desire goes on
Turning inside his body.
He never phrased
What he desired,
And I am
His son.

7.

Prayer for My Father

Your head is still
Restless, rolling
East and west—
That body in you
Insisting on living
Is the old hawk
For whom the world
Darkens. If I
Am not with you
When you die,
That would be grievous
But just. That part
Of you cleaned
My bones more
Than once. But I
Will meet you
In the young hawk
Whom I see
Inside both
You and me.
This young hawk
Guided you
Into the air—
And will guide

You now to
The Lord of Night,
Who will give
You the tenderness
You wanted here.

In the Funeral Home

1.

I missed the hour of your death.
The coffin lid
Lifted shows some
Fall oak leaves sewn
High above
Your winter face.

I have at last some
Leisure near
Your cream-colored hands.
I write down what you did,
Or did wrong, or did
Not do at all.

The funeral director, a kind
Man, says, "I'll
Go upstairs now
With my family. You sit as long
As you like.
No one is here."

ton Public Library
 renewal 847-590-8706
 ip for email notices.
 www.epl.org

due: 2/4/2017,23:59
: Stealing sugar from the castle : se
d poems,
r: Bly, Robert,
ID: 31192020467211
number: 811.54 Bly.R
nt time: 01/07/2017,11:31

due: 1/14/2017,23:59
: Seabiscuit [videorecording (DVD)]
ID: 31192014635492
number: DVD Drama Seabisc
nt time: 01/07/2017,11:31

due: 1/14/2017,23:59
: Tom Horn [videorecording (DVD)]
ID: 31192035061082
number: DVD Drama Tom
ent time: 01/07/2017,11:31

due: 1/14/2017,23:59
: Tinker tailor soldier spy [videorec
ng (DVD)]
ID: 31192014867103
number: DVD Drama Tinker
ent time: 01/07/2017,11:31

due: 1/14/2017,23:59
: Holiday [videorecording (DVD)]
ID: 31192015228180
number: DVD Comedy Cary Grant set
ent time: 01/07/2017,11:31

2.

You spoke often of the Prince
Of Wales, whom
You admired.
He too wanted something
More—and
He had to steal it.

An old man said to me:
"Your father was
The only man
In the whole county
Who read books
During the Depression."

3.

I lay my palm on
Your chest. Your chest
Is thin below
The burial suit,
A chicken's breast
Below my hand.

Do we have time for
Each other now?
Do you have
Time for me? Seeing
Is good, as Marvell
Said, but eyes

Are also for weeping.
As I stand next
To you in your long
Coffin, I see we
Have more time
Than we can use.

A Week After Your Death

I dreamt last night you
Lived nearby, not
Dead at all, but safe
In a blacksmith's storage room,
With bolts and nails in bins
From floor to ceiling.

You came and brought me
An ivory jar,
Holding a precious fluid,
Which I took. I knew it meant
A crisis had come,
But I let you leave.

Later a man pushed open
The door and threw
Your body down, a wizened,
Astonishingly small body—
Rope still tied
Around the neck.

I woke and cried to my wife:
"He didn't die
That way! There was no rope!
All that is wrong!" She
Said, "In
Your dream he did."

When William Stafford Died

Well, water goes down the Montana gullies.
"I'll just go around this rock and think
About it later." That's what you said.
When death came, you said, "I'll go there."

There's no sign you'll come back. Sometimes
My father sat up in the coffin and was alive again.
But I think you were born before my father,
And the feet they made in your time were lighter.

One dusk you were gone. Sometimes a fallen tree
Holds on to a rock, if the current is strong.
I won't say my father did that, but I won't
Say he didn't either. I was watching you both.

If all a man does is to watch from the shore,
Then he doesn't have to worry about the current.
But if affection has put us into the stream,
Then we have to agree to where the water goes.

Gratitude to Old Teachers

When we stride or stroll across the frozen lake,
We place our feet where they have never been.
We walk upon the unwalked. But we are uneasy.
Who is down there but our old teachers?

Water that once could take no human weight—
We were students then—holds up our feet,
And goes on ahead of us for a mile.
Beneath us the teachers, and around us the stillness.

Drinking the Water

When have we had enough?
When we can turn our head,
Say no to the dog-headed,
Furry-nosed, anus-
Eyed goat of duty,
Give payback to God.
Friends, remember no one
Can see his own ears.

Mirabai, night after night
Let herself down castle
Walls on saris to visit
Her lowborn teacher.
When she washed his old
Feet and drank the water,
Any idiot would know
She did not care.

Glimpsing the grave ahead
The body leaps up,
Cries, "What if death
Comes, what if it all ends!"
Let it end—let the sand
And the ocean part,
Let it be, let
Heaven and earth go their ways.

Thoughts in the Cabin

Why do I suddenly feel free of panic?
Here a summer afternoon, wind-
Blown lake, a cabin of strong logs.

I can live and die with no more
Fame; I'd like ground to walk on,
A few books, occasionally a storm.

I know stories I can tell, and I may
Or may not. There is more
To learn: the wind and the screen door.

The granary of images, the Norwegian
Lore, the power of Schmad Razum,
Good or evil, success or failure.

Expect something else from me—
Maybe less—and don't rule out
Misdirection, misinformation.

St. George, the Dragon, and the Virgin

A sculpture made by Bernt Notke in 1489 for Stockholm Cathedral

St. George fights the dragon.
The spiny dragon,
Who lives in the rat-
Filled caves, is losing.
He fights back,
As when a child
Lifts his four
Feet to hold
Off the insane
Parent. The dragon
Hand grasps the wooden
Lance that has
Penetrated his thorny
Chest, but . . .
Too late . . .

And this girlish knight?
Oh I know him.
I read the New
Testament as I lay
Naked on my bed
As a boy.
That solar boy
Rises up radiant
With his forehead-
Eye that sees past
The criminals' gibbet
To the mindful
Towers of the spirit city.

I hate this boy
Whom I have been
Lifting his lance above
The father. Each of us
Has been this harsh
Dragon on his back.
He is Joseph, Grendel,
What we have forgotten,
The great spirit
The alchemists knew of,
Without whom is nothing.

As children, we knew ours
Was a muddy greatness.
How long it took
To break down that horse
So that he would agree
To abet the solar boy.
This earth-handed, disreputable,
Hoarse-voiced one
Is dying, all
Over the world.
And the Virgin?
She prays
On her knees while
This goes on,
As well she might.

MORNING POEMS

1993–1997

Why We Don't Die

In late September many voices
Tell you you will die.
That leaf says it. That coolness.
All of them are right.

Our many souls—what
Can they do about it?
Nothing. They're already
Part of the invisible.

Our souls have been
Longing to go home
Anyway. "It's late," they say.
"Lock the door, let's go." But

The body doesn't agree. It says,
"We buried a little iron
Ball under that tree.
Let's go get it."

Early Morning in Your Room

It's morning. The brown scoops of coffee, the wasp-like
Coffee grinder, the neighbors still asleep.
The gray light as you pour gleaming water—
It seems you've traveled years to get here.

Finally you deserve a house. If not deserve
It, have it; no one can get you out. Misery
Had its way, poverty, no money at least.
Or maybe it was confusion. But that's over.

Now you have a room. Those lighthearted books:
The Anatomy of Melancholy, Kafka's *Letter
To His Father*, are all here. You can dance
With only one leg, and see the snowflake falling

With only one eye. Even the blind man
Can see. That's what they say. If you had
A sad childhood, so what? When Robert Burton
Said he was melancholy, he meant he was home.

Calling Your Father

There was a boy who never got enough.
You know what I mean. Something
In him longed to find the big
Mother, and he leaped into the sea.

It took a while, but a whale
Agreed to swallow him.
He knew it was wrong, but once
Past the baleen, it was too late.

It's okay. There's a curved library
Inside, and those high
Ladders. People take requests.
It's like the British Museum.

But one has to build a fire.
Maybe it was the romance
Novels he burned. Smoke curls
Up the gorge. She coughs.

And that's it. The boy swims to shore;
It's a fishing town in Alaska.
He finds a telephone booth,
And calls his father. "Let's talk."

The Shocks We Put Our Pitchforks Into

The shocks said that winter
Was coming. Each stood there,
Said, "I've given myself away.
Take me. It's over."

And we did. With the shiny tips
Of our forks, their handles so
Healthy and elegant,
We slipped each bundle free,

Gave it to the load.
Each bundle was like
A soul, tucked back
Into the cloud of souls.

That's how it will be
After death—such an abundance
Of souls, all together—
None tired, in the heavy wagon.

Conversation with the Soul

The soul said, "Give me something to look at."
So I gave her a farm. She said,
"It's too large." So I gave her a field.
The two of us sat down.

Sometimes I would fall in love with a lake
Or a pinecone. But I liked her
Most. She knew it.
"Keep writing," she said.

So I did. Each time the new snow fell,
We would be married again.
The holy dead sat down by our bed.
This went on for years.

"This field is getting too small," she said.
"Don't you know anyone else
To fall in love with?"
What would you have said to her?

The Yellow Dot

In memory of Jane Kenyon

God does what she wants. She has very large
Tractors. She lives at night in the sewing room
Doing stitchery. Then chunks of land at mid-
Sea disappear. The husband knows that his wife
Is still breathing. God has arranged the open
Grave. That grave is not what we want,
But to God it's a tiny hole, and he has
The needle, draws thread through it, and soon
A nice pattern appears. The husband cries,
"Don't let her die!" But God says, "I
Need a yellow dot here, near the mailbox."

Three-Day Fall Rain

The three-day
October rain blows
Leaves down. We knew
That life wouldn't last long.

The dock gleams
With oak leaves, cold
Leaves in the boat, leaves
Spotted in the old man grass.

Hardy warned
Us. Jesus in his boat,
Standing, his back turned,
Being rowed to the other shore.

What Jesus Said

The wind blows where it likes: that is what
Everyone is like who is born from the wind.
Oh now it's getting serious. We are the ones
Born from the wind that blows along the plains
And over the sea where no one has a home.
And that Upsetting Rabbi, didn't he say:
"Take nothing with you, no blanket, no bread.
When evening comes, sleep wherever you are.
And if the owners say no, shake out the dust
From your sandals; leave the dust on their doorstep."
Don't hope for what will never come. Give up hope,
Dear friends, the joists of life are laid on the winds.

When Threshing Time Ends

There is a time. Things end.
All the fields are clean.
Belts are put away.
And the horses go home.

What is left endures
In the minds of boys
Who wanted this joy
Never to end.

The splashing of hands,
Jokes and oats:
It was a music
Touching and fervent.

The Bible was right.
Presences come and go.
Wash in cold water.
The fire has moved.

Tasting Heaven

Some people say that every poem should have
God in it somewhere. But of course Wallace Stevens
Wasn't one of those. We live, he said, "in a world
Without heaven to follow." Shall we agree

That we taste heaven only once, when we see
Her at fifteen walking among falling leaves?
It's possible. And yet as Stevens lay dying
He invited the priest in. There, I've said it.

The priest is not an argument, only an instance.
But our gusty emotions say to me that we have
Tasted heaven many times: these delicacies
Are left over from some larger party.

Wallace Stevens and Florence

Oh Wallace Stevens, dear friend,
You are such a pest. You are so sure.
You think everyone is in *your* family.

It is you and your father and Mozart,
And ladies tasting cold rain in Florence,
Puzzling out inscriptions, studying the gold flake.

It is as if life were a visit to Florence,
A place where there are no maggots in the flesh,
No one screaming, no one afraid.

Your job, your joy, your morning walk,
As if you walked on the wire of the mind,
High above the elephants; you cry out but you never fall.

As if we could walk always high above the world,
No bears, no witches, no Macbeth,
No one screaming, no one in pain, no one afraid.

The Waltz

One man I know keeps saying that we don't need
Heaven. He thinks embroidered Russian
Wedding blouses will take the place of angels,
Or windy nights when the crows fly up in front
Of your car will replace all the Psalmists.

He wants us to dance high-hearted, like the Bacchae,
Even if it's a waltz. It's a little awkward;
But if you practice, he says, you can do it.
The hard thing is to try to figure out how
To say goodbye—even just going to the grocery.

Looking at the Stars

I still think about the shepherds, how many stars
They saw. We owe our love of God to these sheep
That had to be followed, or companioned, all night.
One can't just let them run. By midnight

The stars had already become huge talkers.
The Parent sits in her proud Chair, and is punished.
The Dog follows the Hunter. Each time a story ends
There is such a long pause before another begins.

Those of us who are parents, and getting older,
Long, as tonight, for our children to stand
With us, looking at the stars. Here it is,
Eight thousand years later, and I still remember.

Waking on the Farm

I can remember the early mornings—how the stubble,
A little proud with frost, snapped as we walked.

How the John Deere tractor hood pulled heat
Away from our hands when we filled it with gas.

And the way the sun brought light right out of the ground.
It turned on a whole hill of stubble as easily as a single stone.

Breathing seemed frail and daring in the morning.
To pull in air was like reading a whole novel.

The angleworms, turned up by the plow, looked
Uneasy like shy people trying to avoid praise.

For a while we had goats. They were like turkeys
Only more reckless. One butted a red Chevrolet.

When we washed up at noon, we were more ordinary.
But the water kept something in it of the early morning.

What the Animals Paid

The Hampshire ewes standing in their wooden pens,
Their shiny black hooves close to each other,

Had to pay with their wool, with their wombs,
With their eating, with their fear of the dogs.

Every animal had to pay. Horses paid all day;
They pulled stoneboats and the ground pulled back.

And the pigs? They paid with their squealing
When the knife entered the throat and the blood

Followed it out. The blood, steaming and personal,
Paid it. Any debt left over the intestines paid.

"I am what I am." The pig could not say that.
The women paid with their bowed heads, and the men,

My father among them, paid with their drinking.
The demons shouted to him: "Pay to the last drop!"

For Ruth

There's a graceful way of doing things. Birch branches
Curve slightly upward; or the wind brings a few
Snowflakes down, and then joins the night;
Or you leave me a sprig of chervil and no more.

Each morning we have this new chance. We can walk
A few steps behind the others down the mountain;
We can enter a conversation as if we were blessed,
Not insisting on our old way of gaining pity.

There's a way you have of knowing what another
May need ahead of time, before the party
Begins, as smoke sometimes disappears
Downward among branches. And I've learned

From you this new way of letting a poem be.

Conversation with a Monster

A man I knew could never say who he was.
You know people like that. When he met a monster,
He'd encourage the monster to talk about eating
But failed to say that he objected to being prey.

A day goes by; a week; a month; it's summer.
The adolescent wolverines go out scouting;
Crabs lift their claws; the praying mantis
Get religious. This man keeps trying to adapt.

Adopt? Be adopted? It's funny, but those born
From eggs seem not to feel homeless. Something
Pushes them out, and they fly to sea, or swim
Up from the gravel, milkily transparent, and they're gone.

This man went up to monsters and asked to be
Adopted. I've done that often. Reader, are you
Fond of the Jonah story? Say to a monster,
"I may have something for you, but I can't promise."

The Resemblance Between Your Life and a Dog

I never intended to have this life, believe me—
It just happened. You know how dogs turn up
At a farm, and they wag but can't explain.

It's good if you can accept your life—you'll notice
Your face has become deranged trying to adjust
To it. Your face thought your life would look

Like your bedroom mirror when you were ten.
That was a clear river touched by mountain wind.
Even your parents can't believe how much you've changed.

Sparrows in winter, if you've ever held one, all feathers,
Burst out of your hand with a fiery glee.
You see them later in hedges. Teachers praise you,

But you can't quite get back to the winter sparrow.
Your life is a dog. He's been hungry for miles,
Doesn't particularly like you, but gives up, and comes in.

It Is So Easy to Give In

I have been thinking about the man who gives in.
Have you heard about him? In his story
A twenty-eight-foot pine meets a small wind
And the pine bends all the way over to the ground.

"I was persuaded," the pine says. "It was convincing."
A mouse visits a cat, and the cat agrees
To drown all her children. "What could I do?"
The cat said. "The mouse *needed* that."

It's strange. I've heard that some people conspire
In their own ruin. A fool says, "You don't
Deserve to live." The man says, "I'll string this rope
Over that branch, maybe you can find a box."

The Great One with her necklace of skulls says,
"I need twenty thousand corpses." "Tell you what,"
The General says, "we have an extra battalion
Over there on the hill. We don't need all these men."

The Green Cookstove

A lonely man once sat on a large flat stone.
When he lifted it, he saw a kitchen: a green
Enamel range with big claw feet, familiar.
Someone lives in that room, cooking and cackling.

"I saw her once," Virgil said. "She and Helen
Were sisters." Menelaus
Sits by the window, peeling garlic cloves,
And throwing bread crusts to the chickens.

We'll never understand this. Somewhere below
The flat stone of the skull, a carnivorous couple
Lives and plans future wars. Are we innocent?
These wars don't happen by accident—they occur

Too regularly. How often do we lift the plate
At the bottom of our brain and throw some groceries
Down to the kitchen? "Keep cooking,
My dears," we say. "Something good will come of this."

The Russian

"The Russians had few doctors on the front line.
My father's job was this: after the battle
Was over, he'd walk among the men hit,
Sit down and ask: 'Would you like to die on your
Own in a few hours, or should I finish it?'
Most said, 'Don't leave me.' The two would have
A cigarette. He'd take out his small notebook—
We had no dog tags, you know—and write the man's
Name down, his wife's, his children, his address, and what
He wanted to say. When the cigarette was done,
The soldier would turn his head to the side. My father
Finished off four hundred men that way during the war.
He never went crazy. They were his people.

He came to Toronto. My father in the summers
Would stand on the lawn with a hose, watering
The grass that way. It took a long time. He'd talk
To the moon, to the wind. 'I can hear you growing'—
He'd say to the grass. 'We come and go.
We're no different from each other. We are all
Part of something. We have a home.' When I was thirteen,
I said, 'Dad, do you know they've invented sprinklers
Now?' He went on watering the grass.
'This is my life. Just shut up if you don't understand it.'"

The Face in the Toyota

Suppose you see a face in a Toyota
One day, and you fall in love with that face,
And it is Her, and the world rushes by
Like dust blown down a Montana street.

And you fall upward into some deep hole,
And you can't tell God from a grain of sand.
And your life is changed, except that now you
Overlook even more than you did before;

And these ignored things come to bury you,
And you are crushed, and your parents
Can't help anymore, and the woman in the Toyota
Becomes a part of the world that you don't see.

And now the grain of sand becomes sand again,
And you stand on some mountain road weeping.

Two Ways to Write Poems

"I am who I am." I wonder what one has to pay
To say that. I couldn't do it. For years
I thought, "You are who you are." But maybe
You weren't. Maybe you were someone else.

Sam's friend, who loved poetry, played football
In school even though he didn't want to.
He got hit. Later he said to me, "I write poems.
I am who I am . . . but my neck hurts."

How many times I have begun a poem
Before I knew what the main sounds
Would be. We find out. Toward the end
The poem is just beginning to be who it is.

That's all right, but there's another way as well.
One picks the rhyme words, and so the main
Sounds, before one begins. I wonder what
Yeats had to pay in order to do that.

One Source of Bad Information

There's a boy in you about three
Years old who hasn't learned a thing for thirty
Thousand years. Sometimes it's a girl.

This child had to make up its mind
How to save you from death. He said things like:
"Stay home. Avoid elevators. Eat only elk."

You live with this child, but you don't know it.
You're in the office, yes, but live with this boy
At night. He's uninformed, but he does want

To save your life. And he has. Because of this boy
You survived a lot. He's got six big ideas.
Five don't work. Right now he's repeating them to you.

My Doubts on Going to Visit a New Friend

I'm glad that a white horse grazes in that meadow
Outside your kitchen window; even when it rains
There's still someone there. And it rains often
In the mountains.

I have to ask myself what kind of friend I can be.
You'll want to know whether I do dishes,
Or know my share of stories, or any Wallace
Stevens poems by heart.

I know that I won't talk all the time, or steal
Money, or complain about my room,
Or undermine you, or speak disparagingly
Of your family.

I am afraid there'll be a moment when
I fail you, friend; I will turn slightly
Away, our eyes will not meet, and out in the field
There will be no one.

for John

Visiting Sand Island

Somebody showed off and tried to tell the truth
And drank wine and went to bed. Someone
Woke in the night and wanted his children
To walk in the grass on this island under the stars.

Someone was lucky. Someone had eyes and found
Stars. Someone had feet and found grass.
Someone loved thought, and knew things to learn.
Somone could turn in the river and go up or down.

Someone thought he was unlucky, thought he didn't try
To tell the truth. Someone thought his head was dark.
Someone tried to feel as bad as others did; someone
Flapped along the ground to draw the fox to him.

Tell him, friends, that the nest is now gone;
Tell him the little twigs are all dispersed.
Tell him all he has to do is walk under stars.
Tell him the fox has long since eaten his dinner.

A Week of Poems at Bennington

Sunday

The Dog's Ears

A little snow. Coffee. The bowled-over branches,
The wind; it is cold outdoors; but in the bed
It's warm, in the early lamplight, reading poems.

These fingers, so rosy, so alive, move about
This book. Here is my wide-traveling palm,
The thumb that looks like my father's, the wedding ring.

It's time to prepare myself, as a friend suggested,
"Not to be here." It will happen. People will say,
"That day the dish lay empty on the brown table.

"The gold knob shone alone in the dark.
The light came in, and no eyes received it,
And bits of ice hung on the dog's ears."

Monday

When the Cat Stole the Milk

Well there it is. There's nothing to do.
The cat steals the milk and it's gone.
Then the cat steals you, and you're found
Days later, with milk on your face.

That implies that you become whoever
Steals you. The trees steal a man,
And an old birch becomes his wife
And they live together in the woods.

Some of us have always wanted
God to steal us. Then our friends
Would call each other, and print
Posters, and we would never be found.

Tuesday

Being Happy All Night

It's as if the mice stayed warm inside the snow,
As if my cells heard laughing from the Roman vineyards.
Mice slept despite the cruel songs of the stars.
We laughed and woke and sniffed and slept again.

Some people inside my body last night
Married each other just in order to dance.
And Sara Grethe smiled so proudly the men
Kicked their heels on the planks, but kept the beat.

Oh I think it was the books I read long ago.
It's as if I joined other readers on a long road.
We found dead men hanging in a meadow.
We took dew from the grass and washed our eyes.

 for S.B.

Wednesday

The Widowed Friend

for D.H.

I hear rustlings from the next room; and he is ready
To leave. "See you tomorrow." A long line
Of feeling follows him out the door. He carries
On his shoulders—which slope a little—a divorce,

Prosody, marital love as pertinacious
As a bulldog's mouth, a grandfather, grand-
Mother. Land and death weigh him down, so he
Becomes a large man on a thin bridge walking.

If, now, he lives alone, who will hear
The thin cough in the morning, who will hear
The milk hitting the pail when the old man sings?
Who will notice the forty drafts on yellow paper?

It's up to us to see him, call him, and say,
"Stay, friend, be with us, tell me what happened."

Thursday

We Only Say That

"There are so many things to love around here."
We only say that when we want to hint
Something—the day after we notice a woman,
Who waves a hand with her female bravery.

We say, "The icicles are really brilliant today!"
Or, "Let's make fun of other people."
That would bring us closer. Or, "Martha brought
Her dog out into the morning snow."

Her hand reaches up to brush her neck,
Or she puts on her boots. A voice inside us
Says, "Oh a woman! Let's close the door.
Let's flirt and not flirt. Let's play cards and laugh."

Friday

Wounding Others

Well I do it, and it's done.
And it can't be taken back.
There's a wound in my chest
Where I wounded others.

But it will knit, or heal, in time.
That's what you say.
And some that I wounded
Claim: "I am the better for it."

Was it truth-telling or
A thin man with a knife?
The wound will close, or heal
In time. That's what you say.

Saturday

What the Buttocks Think

Don't tell me that nothing can be done.
The tongue says, "I know I can change things."
The toe says, "I have my ways."
The heart is weeping and remembering Eden.

Legs think that a good run will do it.
Tongue has free tickets; he'll fly to heaven.
But the buttocks see everything upside down:
They want you to put your head down there,

Remind the heart it was upside down
In the womb, so that when your mother,
Knowing exactly where she was going,
Walked upstairs, you weren't going anywhere.

Things to Think

Think in ways you've never thought before.
If the phone rings, think of it as carrying a message
Larger than anything you've ever heard,
Vaster than a hundred lines of Yeats.

Think that someone may bring a bear to your door,
Maybe wounded and deranged; or think that a moose
Has risen out of the lake, and he's carrying on his antlers
A child of your own whom you've never seen.

When someone knocks on the door, think that he's about
To give you something large: tell you you're forgiven,
Or that it's not necessary to work all the time, or that it's
Been decided that if you lie down no one will die.

from It's As If Someone Else Is with Me

1.

It's as if someone else is here with me, here in this room
In which I lie. The longing the ear feels for sound
Has given me the sweetness that I confuse with Her.

The joy of being alone, eating the honey of words.
The white-walled room, and Stevens, and the sun.
This is the joy of the soul that has preserved
Itself despite fleas and soap in the lighthearted sun.

One is not alone when one is alone, if She
Is here. It is a She that no one loves, a She
That one loves when one loves what one does love.

5.

I've been thinking about these little adventures
In morning longing—these embarkations,
Excursions in round hideboats on the sea,
Passing over the beings far below.

The deep vowels—perhaps whales—mourn
And sing at their stone table five miles down
On the ocean floor. They mourn some loss.
But the small finny sounds, the *ers* and *ins*

And *ors* and *ings*, mourn as well—we don't
Know what. Perhaps vowels were all created
In a moment of sorrow before creation—
A grief they've not been able to sing in this life.

7.

It's good to remain in bed awhile, and listen
For the *ay* slyly hidden in sequacious,
And scent in summer world the two *er*s.
I especially love the *in* hidden in woodbins.

Am I like the hog snuffling for truffles,
Followed by skimpy lords in oversized furs?
For this gaiety do I need forgiveness?
Does the lark need forgiveness for its blue eggs?

So it's a bird-like thing then, this warming
And hiding of sounds. They are the little low
Heavens in the nest; now my chest feathers
Widen, now I'm an old hen, now I am satisfied.

When My Dead Father Called

Last night I dreamt my father called to us.
He was stuck somewhere. It took us
A long time to dress, I don't know why.
The night was snowy; there were long black roads.

Finally, we reached the little town, Bellingham.
There he stood, by a streetlamp in cold wind,
Snow blowing along the sidewalk. I noticed
The uneven sort of shoes that men wore

In the early Forties. And overalls. He was smoking.
Why did it take us so long to get going? Perhaps
He left us somewhere once, or did I simply
Forget he was alone in winter in some town?

Words the Dreamer Spoke to My Father in Maine

Ocean light as we wake reminds us how dark
Our old house is. That's home. Like Hamlet,
One visit to Wittenberg is enough, and we'll soon be
Back in crazy Denmark. I dreamt I stood

In a machine shop; my dead father stands beside me.
We talk, but his eyes remain on my chest.
I say to him for the first time: "Oh look at me
When we talk." I could see cubbyholes

With dark tools, and a rough floor stained with oil.
Clotted windows, cobwebs, a black vise.
But sunlight outside our windows speaks of ocean
Light, bone light, Labrador light, prairie light.

It's the same light that glints off swords, and shines
From Idaho rivers some days, and from the thin
Face just before death. I say to my father,
"We could be there if we could lift our eyes."

Looking at Aging Faces

Some faces get older and remain who they are. Oh
You can see disappointment there, where parent-teacher
Meetings have affected the chin; or the nose got pushed
To one side by deaths. So many things happen:
People move away, or your mother becomes crazy
And bites the nurse.

Each face had a long time in the womb to decide
How much it would let worldly things affect it,
How often it would turn toward the wall or the woods,
So it didn't have to be seen, how much
It would give in, how stubbornly it would
Hold its own.

Some faces remain whole and radiant. We study them
To find a clue. Aunt Nettie said, "My father
Put on cufflinks every day." Memories like that
Help. One face, as firmly profiled as a hawk,
Used to say: "The world is fair, and if it's not,
I think it is."

For some of us, insults sink in, or the feet
Inherit two roads and lose the way; for others, cold
And hunger come. Some faces change. It's not wrong.
And if you look carefully, you can see,
By glimpsing us just after we wake,
Who we are.

for Bill and Nancy

A Christmas Poem

Christmas is a place, like Jackson Hole. We all agree
To meet there once a year. It has water, and grass for horses;
All the fur traders can come in. We visited the place
As children, but we never heard the good stories.

Those stories only get told in the big tents, late
At night, when a trapper who has been caught
In his own trap, held down in icy water, talks, and a man
With a ponytail and a limp comes in from the edge of the fire.

As children, we knew there was more to it—
Why some men got drunk on Christmas Eve
Wasn't explained, nor why we were so often
Near tears or why the stars came down so close,

Why so much was lost. Those men and women
Who had died in wars for a thousand years,
Did they come that night? Is that why the Christmas tree
Trembled just before we opened the presents?

There was something about angels. *Angels we have
Heard on high Sweetly singing o'er the plains.*
The angels were certain. But we were not
Certain if our family tonight was worthy.

People Like Us

for James Wright

There are more like us. All over the world
There are confused people, who can't remember
The name of their dog when they wake up, and people
Who love God but can't remember where

He was when they went to sleep. It's
All right. The world cleanses itself this way.
A wrong number occurs to you in the middle
Of the night, you dial it, it rings just in time

To save the house. And the second-story man
Gets the wrong address, where the insomniac lives,
And he's lonely, and they talk, and the thief
Goes back to college. Even in graduate school,

You can wander into the wrong classroom,
And hear great poems lovingly spoken
By the wrong professor. And you find your soul,
And greatness has a defender, and even in death you're safe.

The Neurons Who Watch Birds

We have to think now what it would be like
To be old. Some funny little neurons,
Developed for high-speed runners, and quick-
Handed bowmen, begin to get tired. They fire

But then lay down their bows and watch birds.
The kidney cells—"Too much thinking!" the Chinese
Say—look around for help, but the kids have
All gone to the city. Your friends get hit by lightning,

And your enemies live on. This isn't going to get
Better. Crows yelling from the telephone wires
Don't include you in the stories they tell, and they seem
To remember some story that you haven't heard.

What can you do? We'll have to round up
All those little people wandering about
In the body, get them to sit up straight, and study
This problem: How *do* we die?

Bad People

A man told me once that all the bad people
Were needed. Maybe not all, but your fingernails
You need; they are really claws, and we know
Claws. The sharks—what about them?
They make other fish swim faster. The hard-faced men
In black coats who chase you for hours
In dreams—that's the only way to get you
To the shore. Sometimes those hard women
Who abandon you get you to say, "You."
A lazy part of us is like a tumbleweed.
It doesn't move on its own. Sometimes it takes
A lot of Depression to get tumbleweeds moving.
Then they blow across three or four States.
This man told me that things work together.
Bad handwriting sometimes leads to new ideas;
And a careless god—who refuses to let people
Eat from the Tree of Knowledge—can lead
To books, and eventually to us. We write
Poems with lies in them, but they help a little.

Wanting More Applause at a Conference

It's something about envy. I won't say I'm envious,
But I did have certain moods when I was two.
Now of course I can't remember any of that.
I'm happy if another receives some praise or attention

That's really mine. I talk, and the man next to me
Talks, and he gets the applause. Or I am confused
And she makes sense. This is hard to bear.
I bear it, but it causes trouble inside the den.

Is it a mammal problem then? Six teats are palpable
Far inside the wiry fur, and I want more
Than one? Is that it? It is, but such greed
Is mainly a problem for small mammals.

And I am no longer small. Let's call it a mood
When we can't remember. Let's call it a habit
Of opening the mouth when we, who have
Much, want more, even what belongs to the poor.

A Conversation with a Mouse

One day a mouse called to me from his curly nest:
"How do you sleep? I love curliness."

"Well, I like to be stretched out—I like the bones to be
All lined up. I like to see my toes way off over there."

"I suppose that's one way," he said, "but I don't like it.
The planets don't act that way—nor the Milky Way."

What could I say? You know you're near the end
Of the century when a sleepy mouse brings in the Milky Way.

POEMS FROM
EATING THE
HONEY OF WORDS

1999

Poem for Eudalia

When I was twenty-five it was Eudalia
Who saved me. She was the Queen
Of fire and snow. She was the dark
Christian in the ghazals of love.

She mingled the perfume of her breasts
With the alphabet; and forgave young boys.
She was a Cleopatra in the church aisle,
A sprig of chervil on the Archbishop's bed.

I heard Eudalia cry, "Let Jesus leave
His mother and come to me!"
The Judas vines grow from the belly.
The world is light in every dark hair.

Going Home with the World

Well, the world catches us.
One birdcall and we're in
It again. We say to
The world: "Let's go

To your place." The world
Says, "Okay." A necklace
Of ocean shells hangs
On her bedroom wall.

There's a lit sea urchin
On a shelf, and the paws of a tiger.
Well, let's get comfortable!
But soon the absent tiger

Will come—the one who's
Been missing her paws . . .

Elegy for My Mother

The father sits on a chair and looks at the ground.
It will come, my dears. The femur leads
To the kneecap, and New Zealand is not
Far behind. Today is a day in June.

It's spring and I'm free. Curtains stretch
Out before the window like girls on a picnic.
No one's grandmother has died. The boys
Still hold in them the seeds of Roncevaux.

New people have taken over the motel. It's
All right. What right did we have to throw
Tires into the river? Plotinus nursed
Until he was eleven. He saw the Mother

And she is the hardest to see. The hawk mother's
Wingfeathers shine. My mother's soul is gone.
Some invisible sweetness holds the knee
And the kneecap together, and despite Plotinus

Or because of him, the fire in the heart
Continues burning. Her soul lives in the sparkles
Of sunshine in the curtains now and in the wind.
The father sits in a chair and looks at the ground.

The Dog That Pursues Us

Oh well. The man whose head thinks on a pillow,
Filled with goosy down, all night
Knows, or tries to know, if we are
What we say we are. The down says no.

We turn this way and that, trying to escape
Our childhood, which keeps pursuing us.
It's like a dog! And we are the master,
Running on ahead in the high mountain air.

Oh dog, come closer. We've climbed up so
High we've passed the sheep pens; and now
We're dislodging stones. And still the dog
Keeps nosing our feet up the mountain.

There's this desire to go further up the mountain.
Haven't we given enough of ourselves
To the high air? We could climb higher,
But that would only make more work for the dog.

A Dog, a Policeman, and the
Spanish Poetry Reading

Plaza de Santa Ana, Las Palmas

Tonight I heard a small noisy dog barking
As the Macedonian poet gave—in Macedonian—his poem.
A policeman dressed in his cloud-like uniform
Walked slowly toward the dog, saying with his body:
"Leave us now. Go down this little alley.
Important things are happening here—old ladies
Are listening . . . things you wouldn't understand."

Above us on the building front four white women
Entrusted with Justice and Injustice, War and Art,
Hold up their shields as if to say, "On earth
Men only want us to keep them from barking.
Up here we are alone but separate from the dogs."

After a short silence, the loose little dog began
To bark again, ignoring the rhythm of the poets.
A Castilian poet was speaking now in waves—
Probably concealing his bark, as we all do—
The communal words: *la eternidad* and *la muerte*
And *la mar.* The sound of the words suggested—
In some way that none of us could understand—
That we as human beings were better than we are.
They were like a fancy cart carrying us
Away from the orphanage and farther from truth.
Suddenly I admired Antonio Machado even more
Who in his poems had broken this sleep of vowels.
I could see Antonio in a coat slowly climb out
Of the pony cart, and walk back toward the orphanage.

Thinking of *Gitanjali*

A man is walking along thinking of *Gitanjali*,
And a mink leaps out from under a log. I don't know
Why it is I want you to sit on my lap,
Or why it is our children speak to us lovingly.

Answering that is like plotting one's political
Life by listening to Schubert, or letting
The length of your poem be decided by how
Many times the goldfish turns in his bowl.

I do remember that boy in the third grade
Who said, "We're friends, but let's fight!"
So affection intricately inserts itself.
The story makes sense, I guess, like everything

Else that happened when you were
On your way to school. And those gestures
Of love our mother gave us we saved
Somewhere, as Tagore did, until they

Became evidence of the love of God.

Talking into the Ear of a Donkey

I have been talking into the ear of a donkey.
I have so much to say! And the donkey can't wait
To feel my breath stirring the immense oats
Of his ears. "What has happened to the spring,"
I cry, "and our legs that were so joyful
In the bobblings of April?" "Oh, never mind
About all that," the donkey
Says. "Just take hold of my mane, so you
Can lift your lips closer to my hairy ears."

THE NIGHT ABRAHAM CALLED TO THE STARS

2001

The Night Abraham Called to the Stars

Do you remember the night Abraham first saw
The stars? He cried to Saturn: "You are my Lord!"
How happy he was! When he saw the Dawn Star,

He cried, "You are my Lord!" How destroyed he was
When he watched them set. Friends, he is like us:
We take as our Lord the stars that go down.

We are faithful companions to the unfaithful stars.
We are diggers, like badgers; we love to feel
The dirt flying out from behind our back claws.

And no one can convince us that mud is not
Beautiful. It is our badger soul that thinks so.
We are ready to spend the rest of our life

Walking with muddy shoes in the wet fields.
We resemble exiles in the kingdom of the serpent.
We stand in the onion fields looking up at the night.

My heart is a calm potato by day, and a weeping
Abandoned woman by night. Friend, tell me what to do,
Since I am a man in love with the setting stars.

Jerez at Easter

Please tell me why the lamb is in love with the wolf
And why the child's finger calls the hammer down
And why at dusk Alexander walks toward his enemies.

Tell me why the gazelle grazes so close to the lion
And why the rat makes up games on the snake's tail
And why the student bends his head when he's attacked.

One meadow in the redwoods can contain a thousand ferns.
By this we deduce we are living in the serpent's home.
Each curly fern is his tongue unfolding.

The poet makes a meadow from each leaf.
Each curve of language turns into a lamb's ear,
Because a genius is a child in the house of suffering.

None of us is free from a certain bend in the knee.
The caws from the oak-bound ravens in the trees
Around our house guide Alexander toward the night.

The old man's voice breaks as he sings at Easter.
In between the clapping, there's always a voice breaking.
Last night in Jerez some people lived, some people died.

Moses' Cradle

The Pharaoh's wives touch the mud with their toes.
You and I float in Moses' cradle. Dear friends, you and I
Are parted by a thin skin from the ignorance of the Nile.

Ghosts compose themselves from ground mist.
Friends, our souls are moist. "Dry souls are best."
Plotinus thought so, but he was nursing at eleven.

Some children hear the thin words spoken by the dead.
Men piece out secrets hidden in prime numbers.
Women report what Eternity has told them to say.

Our cradle, like Moses', is porous to the Nile.
You and I will never have one whole day of light.
At three o'clock, a wall will creak, or a hare will die.

Beauty has reached us drenched in birth blood.
As our eyes open, bright blood splashes on the floor.
The baby's descent gives us a taste for war.

Some souls remember well, climb so high
They are remembered forever. But Macbeth fell
A thousand miles when the feathers touched his face.

The Dead of Shiloh

"A drowsy numbness pains my sense." Keats heard
The nightingale cry out from the place of war.
It was the thud of the buffalo-killer's gun.

The slant soul loves to play cards in the serpent's house.
The crow arrived only yesterday on Noah's boat
With the mud of Abraham's earth between his toes.

Shiloh was like a drug that hid secretly
Among the rough leaves on the Natchez Trace.
All the drinkers wanted it, and fell asleep.

We value addition and subtraction too much.
Ten thousand Newtons wrapping their equations
Around the serpent's tail can't replace a single lover.

The sunfish flashes light to the reeds below.
Moonlight slips inside the oyster's closed eyes.
The Light of Heaven widens the frog's mouth.

The bobber floats in the shadowy weeds.
But a dark hook hangs farther down.
There is nothing on that hook but "Farewell."

When We Became Lovers

Do you laugh or cry when you hear the poet sing?
"Out of the first warmth of the spring, and out
Of the shine of the hemlocks . . ." It's the hemlocks then,

Swaying above the grasses in the cemetery,
That encourage us in our affair with the world.
We have secret meetings with moss at night.

When the night-singer sang, did you notice the mice
Going by? They leave tracks like the setting stars.
Haven't you heard the grunting of the hollyhocks,

Bringing forth their hairy life by the widow's door?
Gravestones gather up the stray tufts of time
That wind would otherwise scatter in the fields.

You and I have been in love with the moon
Rising for a long time, ever since the day
Our mothers took our hands in the spring field.

That was the day we heard the cry of the hemlocks.
We became lovers then; and our road was decided.
We laughed and cried over the warmth of the spring.

Monet's Haystacks

It's strange that our love of Beauty should lead us to hell.
I caught one glimpse of you, and a moment later
My house and books were all thrown into the fire.

Plato wrote by the light from sharks' teeth.
There is always terror near the Quiet Garden.
If we have come to a bad end, let's blame beauty.

The horses of sorrow are always restless, breaking
Out of fences, trampling the neighbors' garden.
The best odes are written by pirates in the moonlight.

When Monet glimpsed the haystack shining in fall dawn,
Knowing that despair and reason live in the same house,
He cried out: "I have loved God!" And he had.

I walked down the aisles of the grocery weeping.
Gleams of light came off my hair when I saw you
And I found myself instantly under the horses' hooves.

My improvidence was to have been too hopeful.
My improvidence was not to see the fall.
I apologize to those in hell for my disturbances.

What Kept Horace Alive

Men and women spend only a moment in Paradise.
The two lovers watch Charlie Chaplin eat his shoe,
And a moment later find themselves barefooted in the grave.

I know that I wanted more than two years with you.
If my wife had been able to absorb more cruelty,
Perhaps I could have paid the fiery angels to go away.

The dead man lies in bed with his great toe
Sticking up; it is because of his toe
That he could carry the burden of marriage so long.

Sometimes I frighten that boy who sleeps on the ground.
He keeps his head in his arms; all he smells is the hair
That is left behind when the groundhog is eaten.

There are as many groundhogs as there are stars.
Wherever there is a lot of anything, we are in trouble.
It is the generosity of snowflakes that leads us to suicide.

The bats' wings are the Saviours of the mosquitoes;
And the cod long for the net. It was only the certainty
Of death that kept Horace alive so long.

Eudalia and Plato

The Dutch have been growing tulips since 1500.
There are eight thousand tulips in one Dutch field.
Every century is full of lovers; so it's not to worry.

Clouds drift over the sea when the wind blows.
Dickens knew there are lovers even in the Law Courts—
The lovers without lawyers receive vast settlements.

The lovers' books are always open to Inspection.
We can see Romeo and Juliet in the tomb,
And paintings of tiny ships in Divine Waters.

Always the lover's body is saving and spending.
During the day its donkey gathers thousands of pearls.
Then at night it spends all that the earth has saved.

Eudalia will not allow Plato to come near
The Garden of Lovers because Eudalia knows
He, being lofty, is afraid of the glory of ruin.

I know how much ruin love can bring.
But at night I hang around the orchard
Hoping to catch one breath from the lovers' tree.

The Trapdoor

Men and women spend only a moment in Paradise.
Then a trapdoor sends them down to the Lords of Misreason,
Where baby kangaroos carry us all off in their small pouches.

Let's all praise the saints who never mention God!
Why should the leghorn family praise the knife-grinder?
I don't think it's right for water to assist the grindstone, either.

The walls of my poetry house are splashed with blood.
I don't want to be inward. Every day a thousand mice
Run out of my door heading for Tennyson's house.

Arabs with big eyes studied all night for years
And translated the Tablets of the Alchemists.
They could pull Mercury from the knees of the wind.

Jabir the Brilliant at fourteen could arrange
Sounds so they became holy. Friends, each day
I crawl over and kiss some of the books I love.

It is because the lovers have been exiled
To the nonexistence of the onion fields
That the pauper wakes up playing the flute of gratitude.

Hannibal and Robespierre

We saw new ice in the ruts on the way to school.
Once I saw through the ice, even dying sheep
Could not convince me that the world is not right.

The picker missed many ears of corn in the fall.
Later, most of them fell to earth. Those ears
Lay touching the ground the whole winter.

The dove's drunken call rising from the orchard
Where the young lambs stood near their mothers
Convinced me to throw in my lot with the dust.

Please don't insist again on your idea that people
Are bad and animals good. Bees have their hives.
Every old frog is a son of Robespierre.

Our joy was ruined anyway long ago
For the sake of order; the boy's and girl's Delight
Would still be bound even if Rousseau got his way.

Hannibal's elephants never got back to Africa.
We know that the world loses many things. But
Even wars don't mean that the world is wrong.

Walking Backward

Friends, there is only one joy and hundreds of sorrows.
We live down here in the Abode of Smelly Bones
Near the widow's door, near Whitman's retarded brother.

Even though it's dawn on the rooftops, it's still night
Here, among cabbages and shoats, among
Glints from the wings of the mice-seeking owls.

Grown men are often strange. Savonarola
Was uncomfortable in a strawberry patch,
And Aristotle was uneasy beside the generous sea.

Something in mother's milk frightened both
The Italians and Greeks. A drop of milk
Creates a crown when it falls back into milk.

The Sumerians, pressing their stylus into wet clay,
Found their way to the sites of their great
White-walled cities by the smell of milk.

In our messy world, we all walk backward,
Each holding a potato that points to the grave.
The night of infidelity and longing goes on forever.

Wanting to Steal Time

People are moving big milk cans around in
The storeroom, and I am there. Each day I move
Barrels full of nothing to a different spot.

I want to charge you for the rustmarks on my pants.
When greed comes by, I hitch a ride on the truck.
You'll see nothing but my backside for miles.

Every noon as the clock hands arrive at twelve,
I want to tie the two arms together,
And walk out of the bank carrying time in bags.

Don't bother to associate poets with saints
Or extraordinary beings. People like us have already
Hired someone to weep for our parents.

We have a taste for ignorance, and a fondness
For the mediocre dressed up as fame. We love
To go with Gogol looking for dead souls.

Counting up the twelve syllables in a line
Could make us allies of the stern Egyptians
Whose armies were swallowed by the Red Sea.

Calderón

Each mole and shoat is a shadow thrown by the sun.
Each muskrat, each badger, each hedgehog is a shadow.
That's why they can hide so well in the leaves.

Don't comfort me by putting flowers in my room.
Don't quote me the secret poems of Calderón.
Don't mention freedom in the execution room.

Each day I awake, the Lord of Greed senses
A new way to put my head down on the desk.
At a wedding I envy even the minister.

Whichever room I am in, he wants me to be
First, and I agree. So many injustices
Have come into the world through me.

The burning of monasteries is built into
Our world. In every neighborhood you'll find
A Roman general living near Lucretia's house.

There are so many different designs of the snowflake.
There are so many halibut caught in the net.
There are so many salmon tails touching in the dark.

The Wagon and the Cliff

The pin fails, and the wagon goes over the cliff.
The doctor steps out a moment and the boy dies.
We might question Emerson about this moment.

Please don't imagine that only people are greedy.
When a crow lifts off, its ungainly wings
Can carry a thousand Mandelas to the Island.

Hippolytus resisted women a little too much
And the Lady of the Sea decided against him.
His horses agreed to drag him along the stones.

Mourning doves singing from the fenceposts
When I was a boy woke the whole countryside.
But a dove's breastbone is a cathedral of desire.

Sometimes the saints make us seem better than we are.
Our ancestors, on their passport photos, knew
The sound of a bird being pushed out of its nest.

Because I've become accustomed to failure,
Some smoke of sadness blows off these poems.
These poems are windows blown open by winter wind.

Forgiving the Mailman

Let's celebrate another day lost to Eternity.
Minute by minute we eke out the story.
But the spider is on his way from night to night.

The mailman is not the one who ruins our life.
Wind has an affair with a million grains of sand.
Each sand grain has more power than Xerxes.

During those months while we slept in the womb,
The Demiurge gave us a taste for war
So that we were born mortgaged and howling.

Madame Bovary could not endure the good life.
She was like us: she wanted disgraceful nights,
Torn clothes, and the inconstant heart.

Our impoverishment follows naturally from our wealth.
The pain that man and wife feel at breakfast
Each day goes back to decisions in Heaven.

What will you say to Mahler about his daughter
Who died young? There were closed carriages in Vienna.
Freud tried to cure the insufficiency of our sorrow.

The Way the Parrot Learns

I'm afraid to talk to you about my little toe,
Because I know that it will never agree to fasting.
The only ally I have is the sole of my foot.

We all live close to our greedy souls.
We have inherited so many longings
That in the other world our name is "So Many."

One teaspoon of envy was enough for me
To attack Robert Lowell; with a tablespoon
I could have taken on Henry James and Abelard.

Trainers once placed a parrot before a mirror,
And a man behind. The parrot, assuming
A parrot was speaking, would learn to talk.

Perhaps if God would put up a mirror
And sit behind it, and talk, I could believe
That those words of mercy were coming from me.

Why should the rooster go over every detail
Of his beheading? Let's leave some darkness
Around those days when we danced in the road.

Rembrandt's Portrait of Titus with a Red Hat

It's enough for light to fall on one half of a face.
Let the other half belong to the restful shadow,
The shadow the bowl of bread throws on the altar.

Some paintings are like a horse's eating place
At the back of the barn where a single beam
Of light comes down from a crack in the ceiling.

Painting bright colors may lie about the world.
Too many windows cause the artist to hide.
Too many well-lit necks call for the ax.

Beneath his red hat, Titus's eyes hint to us
How puzzled he is by the sweetness of the world—
The way the dragonfly hurries to its death.

So many forces want to kill the young
Male who has been blessed. The Holy Family
Has to hide many times on the way to Egypt.

Titus receives a scattering of darkness.
He's baptized by water soaked in onions;
The father protects his son by washing him in the night.

Nikos and His Donkey

Let's tell the sweet story about the day Nikos,
Wandering around with his donkey and saddlebags,
Turned up one day at a farm of Godseekers.

The Godseekers all came out when he knocked.
They welcomed him, gave him tea, brought
His donkey to the stable for oats and water.

"Stay for supper," they said. How glad he was!
They drank tea for hours. Dinner came.
They all ate happily and began to dance.

The Godseekers sang two lines over and over:
"Compared to God's, our song is only a bray;
How beautiful is the scent of a thousand hairs!"

In the morning, he said, "Could I have my donkey?"
They said: "What do you mean, your donkey?
You ate the meal! You danced. You sang the songs!"

The donkey we have loved for years may be killed
And cooked one day while we go on singing.
Let's not write a single poem without gratitude.

Pitzeem and the Mare

Let's tell the other story about Pitzeem and his horse.
When the One He Loved moved to the mountains,
He bought a mare and a saddle and started out.

He rode all day with fire coming out of his ears,
And all night. When the reins fell, the mare knew it right
Away. She turned and headed straight for the barn.

No one had told Pitzeem, but his horse had left
A new foal back in the stable. She thought of nothing
All day but his sweet face with its long nose.

Pitzeem! Pitzeem! How much time you've lost!
He put the mountain between the mare's ears again.
He slapped his own face; he was a good lover.

And every night he fell asleep once more. Friends,
Our desire to reach our true wife is great,
But the mare's love for her child is also great. Please

Understand this. The journey was a three-day trip,
But it took Pitzeem thirty years. You and I have been
Riding for years, but we're still only a day from home.

The Country Roads

Last night in my dream, I drank tea steeped
In iron that had failed; at the bottom
I saw ruined tines of an old pitchfork.

Everything we leave behind is testimony,
Even our nail-clippings. Then my old clothes
Are testimony of my love of nakedness.

During the months everyone spoke badly of us,
Then I had the fiercest love for you.
People still try to encourage us by speaking badly.

So many times this week I've felt like weeping.
It's natural, like the cry of Canada Geese
Who call to each other over the darkening reeds.

In my early poems I praised so many lost things.
The way the crickets' cries in October carried
Them into the night sky felt right to me.

Every way of knowing is blessed by bootleggers.
Because the government does not allow delight
To be sold, you have to find it on the country roads.

In Praise of Scholars

Furry shadows are bringing gifts to our door.
We have nowhere to live but with the moles.
We'll have to pay the mortgage in the house of sorrow.

This world is roofed with the shingles of parting.
Children slide off their mothers' knees;
The door leads inward to silent wives and husbands.

All his life my father wrote figures down
With a short, blunt pencil. Even Aristotle
Found himself caught in his dark reason.

It's too late to move now, friends. We'll have to pay
For years—yes!—and the interest rate is fixed.
It will require our lives, as it did our parents'.

Hundreds of scholars work in the basement.
They are good students of the ten thousand things.
Without them we would be at war forever.

There is only one mortgage and so many forms of payment!
There is one peace and so many forms of war.
The furry shadows are bringing gifts to the door.

The Fish in the Window

"The fish are in the fishman's window," the grain
Is in the hall, "the hunter shouts as the pheasant falls."
That shout rises from deep in Adam's chest.

The great trawlers pull in the shining bodies.
Horses' teeth rip night from sleepy day.
We are all like Nebuchadnezzar on his knees.

Because the greedy soul gained its teeth in the womb,
More than one twin died in the safest place;
We fell into the doctor's hands with haunted eyes.

We inherited much when we inherited teeth.
We will never have one whole day of peace.
An old horse will die or a house will burn.

Each evening we reach for our neighbor's food.
Each night we crawl into imaginary beds;
Each midnight we visit the darkness with Saturn.

We can go on sitting in the Meeting House,
But the greedy one in us will still survive.
One cry from the crow contains a thousand more.

Montserrat

Why God allowed Montserrat to fall
Is not explained, nor why the Queen of Cattle
Drove my one calf into the slaughterhouse.

My poems are sad. How could it be otherwise?
The judge and the criminal live in my own house.
I come constantly upon secret court proceedings.

Why do we achieve organization only in wartime?
I want to know why so many plays of Sophocles were lost,
And why God becomes an ox and eats the grass each night.

When I was twenty-six, I sent the words that fed me
To be killed, along with vowels that joined me to others;
My calf of language was cut up and thrown into the ditch.

My small talent was weighted down beneath the water,
And the lungs I breathed with were filled with lies.
If I had been human, it would have been worse.

Robert, you've been complaining enough now.
All this about Sophocles is too much.
Pack up your suffering and go home.

The French Generals

Whenever Jesus appears at the murky well,
I am there with my five hundred husbands.
It takes Jesus all day to mention their names.

The growing soul longs for mastery, but
The small men inside pull it into misery.
It is the nature of shame to have many children.

Earth's name is "Many, Many, Many." The serpent
Sends out his split tongue and waves it
In the air scented with many dark Napoleons.

The general ends his life in a small cottage
With damp sheets and useless French franc notes;
He keeps his old plans of attack under the mattress.

I say to the serpent: "This is your house."
I bring in newspapers to make his nest cozy.
It's the nature of wanting to have many wives.

So many rafters in life jackets are pulled down.
So many boats are turned over at night.
Wherever there is water there is someone drowning.

The Battle at Ypres, 1915

Tammuz, bright with feathers, goes to the Underworld.
The peat-bog man sleeps on his slanted face.
Not to worry; it means that spring has come.

Naked men crawl into tunnels to retrieve the giant
Snakes. They don't resist if pulled out backwards.
Ah, friends, the world pulls us out backwards.

Some say that every bit of iron we pull
Out of the earth, and shape, we have to pay for.
At Ypres we paid dearly for the Bentley car.

Some greedy part hankers for disaster, for things
To go wrong, for the war to start. Many people
Are disappointed when the bombing is canceled.

Events at times turn out exactly wrong with us.
The Magi are misled by a satellite in the night;
And a rabbit sacrifices people during our Easter.

Our gaiety the morning of war is momentary.
Soon we have entered some disaster.
The stars will not save us this time either.

for Martín Prechtel

The Raft of Green Logs

Poetry is an occupation fit for slaughterers
And knife-wielders. Life on earth needs many kills
To engender the soft leaps of the cheetah.

God made me tender; but writing poetry,
With its whole herd of images that have
To be saved or murdered, has made me fierce.

The Lord of this World condemns half his friends
To death. Music testifies to that. Notes
Wave their arms and sink into the cold Atlantic.

During the years I called to Rilke and Boehme,
I hung on to small branches; I went over
The waterfall still holding the twig of reason.

It's all right if we tumble down the falls.
I remember how many lambs died on the farm.
Our desires reform themselves overnight anyway.

My affections were stuffed into the giant's mouth.
Some marriages are rafts. I saw water between
The green logs. You could not have saved me.

The Baal Shem and Francis Bacon

"The Five Ways of Knowing the World" worry me.
The thrush has so many tiny feathers around its bill
That a thousand ways of knowing might be closer.

Some old souls living in the Divine House felt
Such fear at the amount of darkness God
Left inside man during the Second Creation,

That they hid themselves away in an inner room,
And never looked down at those tall grasses
Where Adam sat killing rabbits by the first fire.

When the Baal Shem was about to be born,
His soul was chosen from among that group of souls
Who had turned their eyes away from the window.

That's why the Baal Shem could travel a hundred
Miles in two hours and arrive just in time
To give the poor daughter money for her marriage.

That's why Francis Bacon could never understand
How the world allows itself to be loved, nor how
Joseph's shirt could come back from Egypt.

Natchez Inns

Let's just stay here weeping over old grain.
We've spent hours asleep, and other hours,
Dozens of them, hitched to the black horse.

We love most those hours that carry the burnt flavor
Of the stars; but we have to have praised God
For hours before the burnt minute appears.

Whenever we set a foot down, it is caught.
The steps we take resemble those Natchez inns
Where each pillow covers an open knife.

The bird can sing for hours through its beak!
It picks its grain carefully. But we, the sons
Of forgetfulness, eat the flesh that died shouting,

We have to fight the Agent of Disappointment a year
To love one disappearing star for a moment, because
Any star may carry us close to Orion's Belt.

Be frank with me: Tell me how many dead hours
You have eaten, whom you have killed
While waiting for the Lord of this planet to fall asleep.

The Cabbages of Chekhov

Some gamblers abandon carefully built days
In order to live near water. It's all right.
One day on the river is worth a thousand nights.

It is our attraction to ruin that saves us;
And disaster, friends, brings us health. Chekhov
Shocks the heavens with his dark cabbages.

William Blake knew about that fierce man,
Irritable, chained, and majestic, who bends over
To measure with his calipers the ruin of the world.

It takes so little to make me happy tonight!
Four hours of weeping will do it, if we remember
How much of our life is a ruin, and agree with that.

Butterflies spend all afternoon concentrating
On the Buddleia bush; human beings take in
The fragrance of a thousand nights of ruin.

We planted fields of sorrow near the Tigris.
The Harvesters will come in at the end of time
And report that the crop of ruin has been great.

The Eel in the Cave

Our veins are open to shadow, and our fingertips
Porous to murder. It's only the inattention
Of the prosecutors that lets us go to lunch.

Reading my old letters I notice a secret will.
It's as if another person had planned my life.
Even in the dark, someone is hitching the horses.

That doesn't mean I have done things well.
I have found so many ways to disgrace
Myself, and throw a dark cloth over my head.

Why is it our fault if we fall into desire?
The eel poking his head from his undersea cave
Entices the tiny soul falling out of Heaven.

So many invisible angels work to keep
Us from drowning; so many hands reach
Down to pull the swimmer from the water.

Even though the District Attorney keeps me
Well in mind, grace allows me sometimes
To slip into the Alhambra by night.

Rembrandt's Etchings

The cross-hatching brings the night into the day,
Just as the donkey brings its cargo into Egypt.
I am a beggar reaching out my hand for darkness.

The cat can't explain how much the mouse loves
Its teaspoon of darkness; nor we why we sip
So thirstily from the pond made with a sharp stylus.

What is this? A monk and a girl in the corn?
He can no more keep his seed from rising
Than the kernel prevent the corn from coming up.

The resting hog is content, tied by one leg,
At least for now. She is far down on the earth;
And no longer remembers small boys or boiling water.

Joseph needs a lantern as he and Mary
Travel silently through the night. The donkey
Is about to put its hoof down in that darkness.

There is nothing more to say. The road to Egypt
Is long; there are enemies on all sides.
And the hatching and shadowiness are everywhere.

The Cardinal's Cry

The cardinal's cry could be heard at Gettysburg.
Some stars have no choice but to set in the west.
It's always night in the grain-bin of birth.

Vintners made strong red wine from the battlefields
Where the Romans died; and we know that hundreds
Of mothers loved the buffalo-killers' hands.

Every poem is a cover over something naked.
Emily Dickinson's poems are shawls woven
From the lengthened hair of the ignorant and insane.

Ducks are swimming in and out of the reeds
In the marshy lakes of the amygdala.
A hunter shoots at everything that flies by.

The tumbling of clowns is part of the abundance
That gives birth to death, along with bitter
Berries, charcoal, and the first snow.

The muddler you are reading has lied to you
Often because he didn't want to see how many
Things cannot be saved even if Abraham returns.

The Old St. Peter by Rembrandt

Noah's ship does not sail with its elephants forever.
The crying of the monkeys breaks off and starts again.
Even shame does not last a whole lifetime.

"It was dark," Peter said. "We were alone. We had
A single candle which shone on the steel breastplate
Of the Roman soldier. The whole town was asleep."

We are bubbles on the lips of our friends.
Each time they turn their heads, we drift toward the Pole;
We pass into the Many and return.

Who can say, "With God, the rest is nothing"?
Who can say, "I am a grandchild of the unfaithful"?
Who is able to wait one month to drink water?

We fell into weeping yesterday at five o'clock.
We wept because slavery has returned; we wept
Because the whole century has been a defeat.

Oh Peter! Peter! The night behind you is black.
A beam of light falls on your outworn face.
What can you do but lift up your hand for forgiveness?

Chicago Museum of Art

Why Is It the Spark's Fault?

The soul is in love with marshy ground and snails,
With mud, darkness, wind, smoke and fire.
The cucumber and melon lead us back toward Heaven.

Why is it the spark's fault if the moment a hammer
Hits hot iron the spark curves toward earth?
In July even lightning cannot help itself.

Italian fiddlers are always ready to play
Near the enclosed bed of the Prodigal Son
While a plump woman cuts a pear with a small knife.

Let's keep disaster remembered in our poems.
Our memory feeds on ruin just as cows
Stand around drinking from river water.

Who stands for the melon? Seth, Abraham,
And Shem. The lightness of grasshoppers suggests
They are taking in some fiddle music from the grass.

Please forgive me if I know so many words
And say so little. The Word catches in my throat,
Because some force does not want me to follow Abraham.

Augustine on His Ship

Each time we lower a violin near the Nile River,
The low G string cries; it's like the cry a ribbon
Makes when a raven carries it into his nest.

No one knows what the jaguar's whisker feels
Immersed in the bath water of St. Francis.
We each have to be careful talking of our betters.

How can the literalists with their heavy voices
Speak through the thin bill of the thrush, or the spark,
Alone in wet cow dung, call to its friends?

So much flesh muffles the slow bones
Of the beaver that it's difficult for light
To pass from the tip of the tail to the skull.

Perhaps that's why Rimbaud whose gold tooth
Was so delicately tuned to the Milky Way
Of language could still die as a slave trader.

Every fall the Kraken comes up and brushes
With his Gnostic arms the hull of the ship
On whose planks Augustine walks at night.

The Difficult Word

The oaks reluctantly let their leaves fall,
And hesitatingly allow their branches to be bare;
And the Bear spends all winter in separation.

The beauty of marriage is such that it dissolves
All earlier unions, and leads man and wife
To walk together on the road of separation.

The word is a difficult one. The thought frightens us
That this planet with all its darkening geese
Was created not for union but for separation.

Suppose there were a dragon curled inside each drop
Of water, defending its gold. It's possible
That abundance has the same effect as separation.

Each of us was glad floating in the loopy
Joy of the womb; but when our lips touched
Our mother's breast, we said, "This is separation."

It is my longing to smooth the feathers
Of birds and touch the hair of horses for hours
That has led me to spend my life in separation.

The Storyteller's Way

It's because the storytellers have been so faithful
That all these tales of infidelity come to light.
It's the job of the faithful to evoke the unfaithful.

Our task is to eat sand, our task is to be sad,
Our task is to cook ashes, our task is to die.
The grasshopper's way is the way of the faithful.

Even though you are a literalist, accept
The invitation to go to Pluto's wedding.
Haven't you learned yet that the stars are faithful?

For every planet, there are a million jellyfish
Shooting along who don't know night from morning.
So is the sea full of the unfaithful or the faithful?

A storyteller has to remember every turn
Of language so that we all know the moment
When the King decides to betray the faithful.

My whole life makes clear that I am a prodigal
Who loves the violin most in the doubtful inns.
I am unfaithful even about being unfaithful.

for Gioia Timpanelli

How This Wealth Came to Be

It's hard to know how all this wealth came to the world.
Ishmael was not created from a fight with a whale.
The ocean is not deep enough to have created Melville's soul.

The hungry one in us did not come from our seed.
Our old enemy is one of Adam's grandfathers.
He stood around looking at the shadow of the first soul.

The Ark floated for months; but all those
Who came off the Ark know that Mount Ararat
Was not high enough to produce Abraham's soul.

Oaks once darkened almost all of Great Britain,
Covering it with leaves. But squirrels rummaging
In a million acorns could not find Chaucer's soul.

Do you know how many boulders had to be ground
Down to produce one square inch of the Sahara?
Maybe the moon gave birth to Mandela's soul.

There is a mystery about the birth of Jesus.
All the snow that fell to earth on Christmas Eve
Finally did shift the weight of Rome's soul.

Noah Watching the Rain

I never understood that manyness leads to war,
Nor that stones are like gasoline on the fire.
I never knew that the horseshoe longs for night.

All through my twenties I worked in the opal mines.
No one could open the door to Saturn's house.
I had no choice but to live in my father's night.

I am still a mouse nibbling the chocolate of sadness.
I am an Albigensian reading Bulgarian script.
I am a boy walking across England by night.

Each time we fold in the fingers of our left hand
We bring our ancestors close to each other again,
So they can lie on top of each other in the bed at night.

Soon our grandfather and grandmother will kiss
Once more. Then death will come in his Jewish hat,
And tell Noah to start praising the rainy night.

Even though I know that whenever I say the word
Abundance, I am laying up trouble for ourselves,
I have no other way to express my love for the night.

Listening

The goose cries, and there is no way to save her.
So many cheeps come from the nest by the river.
If God doesn't listen, why are we listening?

Very deep water covers most of the globe.
Whenever I see it, I think of St. John.
There is no remedy for deep water but listening.

The King and Queen already know about love;
They search for each other through the whole deck.
While we play our hands, they are listening.

The day we die, we'll each be like the fish
Abruptly jerked out of the water.
For him, it is the end of all listening.

Like thousands of others, I'm eating beet soup
In some Russian inn. People write letters
To me from heaven, but I'm not listening.

The hermit said: "Because the world is mad,
The only way through the world is to learn
The arts and double the madness. Are you listening?"

So Be It. Amen.

There are people who don't want Kierkegaard to be
A humpback, and they're looking for a wife for Cézanne.
It's hard for them to say, "So be it. Amen."

When the disciples found a dead dog on the road,
They held their noses. Jesus walked over and said:
"What beautiful teeth!" It's a way to say Amen.

If a young boy leaps over seven hurdles in a row,
And an instant later is an old man reaching for his cane,
To the swiftness of it all we have to say Amen.

We always want to intervene when we hear
That the badger is marrying the wrong person,
But the best thing to say at a wedding is Amen.

The grapes of our ruin were planted centuries
Before Caedmon ever praised the Milky Way.
Praise God, Damn God are all synonyms for Amen.

Women in Crete loved the young men, but when
"The Son of the Deep Waters" dies in the bath,
And they show the rose-colored water, Mary says Amen.

Dawn

Some love to watch the sea bushes appearing at dawn,
To see night fall from the goose wings, and to hear
The conversations the night sea has with the dawn.

If we can't find Heaven, there are always bluejays.
Now you know why I spent my twenties crying.
Cries are required from those who wake disturbed at dawn.

Adam was called in to name the Red-Winged
Blackbirds, the Diamond Rattlers, and the Ring-Tailed
Raccoons washing God in the streams at dawn.

Centuries later, the Mesopotamian gods,
All curls and ears, showed up; behind them the generals
With their blue-coated sons who will die at dawn.

Those grasshopper-eating hermits were so good
To stay all day in the cave; but it is also sweet
To see the fenceposts gradually appear at dawn.

People in love with the setting stars are right
To adore the baby who smells of the stable, but we know
That even the setting stars will disappear at dawn.

MY SENTENCE
WAS A THOUSAND
YEARS OF JOY

2005

The Dark Autumn Nights

Imagination is the door to the raven's house, so we are
Already blessed! The one nail that fell from the shoe
Lit the way for Newton to get home from the fair.

Last night I heard a thousand holy women
And a thousand holy men apologize at midnight
Because there was too much triumph in their voices.

Those lovers, skinny and badly dressed, hated
By parents, did the work; all through the Middle Ages,
It was the lovers who kept the door open to Heaven.

Walking home, we become distracted whenever
We pass apple orchards. We are still eating fruit
Left on the ground the night Adam was born.

St. John of the Cross heard an Arab love poem
Through the bars and began his poem. In Nevada it was
Always the falling horse that discovered the mine.

Robert, you know well how much substance can be
Wasted by lovers, but I say, Blessings on those
Who go home through the dark autumn nights.

Listening to the Sitar Before Dawn

It is not yet dawn, and the sitar is playing.
Where are the footsteps that were so clear yesterday?
Sometimes stones have no weight at all, and clouds are heavy.

To those who want me to change, I say, "I will
Never stop traveling that road which connects
Socrates to the turtle, and Falstaff to the Baal Shem."

Every sitar note strikes a bargain with the one
Who arranges things. One note says, "A year in Heaven."
The turgid silence says, "Two years under the earth."

The sitar players are already pulling Heaven down,
While we have hardly learned to carry earth.
Perhaps they remember all their errors in loving.

Some say that Ganesha and Catherine do the work
For us all, but I see a great deal of faithfulness
In the dragonfly with her long, skinny body.

It was still dark when the fingers began to play.
Now we who have listened so hard have nothing to say.
The wavering sitar note is the early dawn.

 for David Whetstone

Loafing with Friends at Ojo Caliente

Mineral pools remember a lot about history.
Here we are at Ojo Caliente, sitting together,
Soaking up the rumble of earth's forgetfulness.

Why should we worry if *Anna Karenina* ends badly?
The world is reborn each time a mouse
Puts her foot down on the dusty barn floor.

Sometimes *ohs* and *ahs* bring us joy. When
You place your life inside the vowels, the music
Opens the doors to a hundred closed nights.

People say that even in the highest heaven
If you managed to keep your ears open
You would hear angels weeping night and day.

The culture of the Etruscans has disappeared.
So many things are over. A thousand hopes
F. Scott Fitzgerald had for himself are gone.

No one is as lucky as those who live on earth.
Even the Pope finds himself longing for darkness.
The sun catches on fire in the lonely heavens.

for Hanna and Martín

When I Am with You

When I am with you, two notes of the sarod
Carry me into a place where I am not.
All the farms have disappeared into air.

Those wooden fenceposts I loved as a boy—
I can see my father's face through their wood,
And through his face the sky as threshing ends.

It is such a blessing to hear that we will die.
Ten thousand barks become a hundred thousand;
I knew this friendship with myself couldn't last forever.

Touch the sarod's string once more, so that the finger
That touched my skin a moment ago
Can become a lightning bolt that closes the door.

Now I know why I keep hinting at the word *you*—
The sound of you carries me over the border.
We disappear the same way a baby is born.

Some foolish boy with my name has been trying
To peer all afternoon between the thick boards
Of the fence. Tell that boy it isn't time.

There Are So Many Platos

The mourning dove insists there is only one morning.
The nail remains faithful to its first board.
The hoarse crow cries out to a thousand planets.

The sun goes down through ghettos of clouds.
There is one Burning Mind and so many Platos.
The Morning Star rises over a flutter of wings.

To those who make up music, and write poems,
I say: Our task is to become a moist tongue
By which subtle ideas slip into the world.

Probably we *were* born too near the potato bin.
Like the potato, we have many closed eyes.
A touch on the thigh displaces all the heavens.

There are more planets than have ever been found.
They rise and set again. Some people say
A painting is a pitcher full of the invisible.

Robert, some images in this poem are just right.
It is probably as good as anyone can do
Who is still living in the old inn of desire.

Bach's B Minor Mass

The old Germans step inside Trinity Church.
The tenors, and sopranos, and altos and the horns
Say: "Do not be troubled. Death will come."

The basses reach down into their long coats
And give bits of dark bread to the poor, saying,
"Eat, eat, in the shadow of Jethro's garden."

We all know about the old promise
That the orphans will be fed. The oboes say,
"Oh, that promise is too wonderful for us!"

Don't worry about the sea. The tidal wave that
Wipes out whole cities is merely the wood thrush
Lifting her wings to catch the morning sun.

We know that God gobbles up the Faithful.
The Harvesters on the seafloor are feeding
All of those ruined by the depth of the sea.

Our oak will break and fall. Even after their tree
Has splintered and fallen in the night, once
Dawn has come, the birds can do nothing but sing.

The Blind Tobit

Why does the prophet climb on the same ship so many times?
Why does the sleeper visit other continents by night?
The ship breaks up, and Kafka is lost so many times.

The high school teacher's ghost waits by the stone wall.
Why does the ear always stretch toward the storm?
The Pharaoh imprisons and releases Joseph so many times.

Tobit! Tobit! Your eyes are milky white! Every
Father is blind when his son knocks on the door.
The blind Tobit fumbles for the door so many times.

Why do those who died by the stone wall at Gettysburg
Throw themselves against the Germans at Stalingrad?
The novelist writes and rewrites his novel so many times.

The general fights the same war again and again.
The violinist plays the same toccata over and over.
The conductor conducts the same piece so many times.

Why do some love affairs resemble a blow of lightning?
Are you surprised how often Zoroaster is reborn?
The snow blocks the country roads so many times.

Visiting the Teacher

I am the grandchild of Norwegian forgetters.
I am a nephew of those who stole the onions.
We are all guests at the criminal's wedding.

Each time we pick up a fallen wren's nest,
We sense despair and injustice, but we love to feel
The little crackling of the abandoned eggshells.

To drink a drop of water increases our thirst.
Black-and-white movies intensify our longing
That night will come and simply take over from day.

The shadowy cave we live in extends far out
Over the world. It's dark there. Even Amundsen
And all his dogs couldn't find the end of it.

Stars have set so often in the woods without
Bringing the Magi, that the badger drinks
Sadness each time his nose touches the water.

Last night I brought my grief to my teacher.
I asked him what he could do about it.
He said, "I thought you came because you liked me!"

for Dr. Nurbaksh

Growing Wings

It's all right if Cézanne goes on painting the same picture.
It's all right if juice tastes bitter in our mouths.
It's all right if the old man drags one useless foot.

The apple on the Tree of Paradise hangs there for months.
We wait for years and years on the lip of the falls;
The blue-gray mountain keeps rising behind the black trees.

It's all right if I feel this same pain until I die.
A pain that we have earned gives more nourishment
Than the joy we won at the lottery last night.

It's all right if the partridge's nest fills with snow.
Why should the hunter complain if his bag is empty
At dusk? It only means the bird will live another night.

It's all right if we turn in all our keys tonight.
It's all right if we give up our longing for the spiral.
It's all right if the boat I love never reaches shore.

If we're already so close to death, why should we complain?
Robert, you've climbed so many trees to reach the nests.
It's all right if you grow your wings on the way down.

Tightening the Cinch

Hurry, for the horses are galloping along the road.
Our death is being saddled now. They are tightening the cinch.
Just keep shouting, "My heart is never bitter!"

Come, only a moment is left, the sun is touching
The sea at Point Lobos; those waves that Jeffers knew
Will soon wear the Lincolnish coats of night!

You've waited so long for me. And where was I?
Whatever pleases the greedy soul is like a drop
Of burning oil to the heart. What shall we do?

While they saddle the horses, just keep shouting,
"My grief is a horse; I am the missing rider!"
The grief of absence is the only bread I eat.

Whatever pleases the heart is like a drop of burning
Oil to the greedy soul, which can't bear one moment
When men and women are tender with each other.

You know the writer of this poem has a thin
Hold on the reins, and is about to fall off.
Hold on. The horses are galloping toward the night.

Call and Answer

August 2002

Tell me why it is we don't lift our voices these days
And cry over what is happening. Have you noticed
The plans are made for Iraq and the ice cap is melting?

I say to myself: "Go on, cry. What's the sense
Of being an adult and having no voice? Cry out!
See who will answer! This is *Call and Answer*!"

We will have to call especially loud to reach
Our angels, who are hard of hearing; they are hiding
In the jugs of silence filled during our wars.

Have we agreed to so many wars that we can't
Escape from silence? If we don't lift our voices, we allow
Others (who are ourselves) to rob the house.

How come we've listened to the great criers—Neruda,
Akhmatova, Thoreau, Frederick Douglass—and now
We're silent as sparrows in the little bushes?

Some masters say our life lasts only seven days.
Where are we in the week? Is it Thursday yet?
Hurry, cry now! Soon Sunday night will come.

The Blinding of Samson

Don't you see them? They are coming to blind Samson!
But some of us don't want the day to end!
If Samson goes blind, what will happen to the sea?

Isn't it bad enough that the sun goes down
Each night, while children throw shoes at the moon?
I remember my mother's grief at sunset.

Now I remember my father. I remember
Every father when he is wrestling with his son.
Oh Lord of the Four Quarters—he is destined to lose!

You gypsy singers, make some raw cries!
Call in the crows to fly over the plowed fields.
I want the beating palms to cry out for Samson.

I want rough voices and shouting women
To cry out against the blinding of Samson.
I will always cry—take away those knives!

Isn't it enough that the Evening Star sets every night
And lovemaking ends at dawn? Please, God, help
The human beings, for men are coming to blind Samson.

The Pelicans at White Horse Key

Occasionally spreading their wings to the sun, pelicans
Dive for fish from dawn to dusk. The Lord of This World
Is a painter working at night in a dark room.

Earth is the place where we've agreed to throw
Away the gifts that Adam's grandfather gave us
During the Dark Time before eternity was born.

The lover's body belongs to ruined earth.
The scattered stars belong to the Milky Way.
The potato field belongs to early night.

The Monitor Lizard is a child of the Mother,
And a favorite child. The Monitor holds a snake
Immobile for an hour and then eats.

We know it's good not to have sharp opinions;
But would you still think so much of Noah
If he had thrown away his bag of nails?

Four times this month I have dreamt I am
A murderer; and I am. These lines are paper boats
Set out to float on the sea of repentance.

The Horses Coming Up Behind

Have you noticed the horses galloping past us?
Perhaps they are horses with no riders at all.
Perhaps they are riders who have turned into horses.

A world without horses coming up behind us
Seems absurd to me now. Ride faster!
Why did I let so many centuries go by?

You know how difficult it is at birth to receive
A human body these days! Don't lose this chance!
Clamp your legs tight against the saddle.

You've given me a bridle and a saddle and a horse
That can go on for miles. But it's always possible
That I am the rider destined to lose the race.

It doesn't matter now. We don't care whether
Anna and Vronsky find their way home or not,
Because there is so much joy in losing the race.

So many superb riders have already run this course!
Look at all these riders on fast horses
Going by with their thin cheekbones in the night!

Jacob and Rachel

The harsh bark on the calendar oaks and the bowl
Of milk spilled on the floor tell us that the lover
Long-parted will arrive too late for the funeral.

We'll never be able to remedy the wounds
That Columbus made in the sea; how could we keep
All the promises we've made to the dark angels?

The Egyptian teacher keeps asking why the dead man
Reaches for the wrong Bible, why the pelican
Mistakes her nest on the morning of Easter.

Jacob will fly once more for seven years toward
Rachel's shawl; once more he'll set spotted twigs
At the spring where the ewes drink at nightfall.

Put more sugar into the watercolorist's tea!
Don't forbid the horses to gallop into the storm!
Please keep all frogs alive in the hill pond!

There are so many mistakes in creation we cannot
Correct. As parents, we may never be able to say
The true blessing we want to give to our children.

for Bridget and Ben

What to Do with the Garden

I'll just stay here. You go on. Leave me behind
In this wrecked garden that Joseph forgot to tend.
I have been here since my mother first laid out my clothes.

A group of women keep reminding me whom I love.
They stand with lifted arms in the orchard. They say,
"Leave this ruined garden you love so much."

I believe repentance no larger than a county
Can become a continent of forgiveness.
I believe the Seal has not been set on this door.

Perhaps even my feeble faith may gain me
Mercy. I do believe a pebble on the road
Can throw a shadow a hundred miles long at dusk.

Because I'm absent when I'm present, and present
When I'm absent, because I drop my eyes to the floor,
I've had seventy years living in this ruined garden.

Robert, give up your longing for a different childhood.
You'll recall that Fabre when he was seventy
Found for his insects one acre of stony ground.

The Shoehorn

It's odd that the shoehorn has been able to preserve
Its shape over centuries. At dusk my ignorance
Slips away and hides its eggs in the woods.

Everyone knows when a great man or woman
Is about to die, and fights that. Many of the Jews
Wanted to speak privately to Pilate.

Our parents' faces at dawn have so much grief
That they resemble those stone faces on Easter
Island, gazing toward some missing Friday.

After every one of our wars, the newly dead
Hold out a cup to us. What can we do
But testify to a thousand years of darkness?

Iron keeps calling to earth, and earth to iron.
If you throw a knife high in the air,
The knife soon curves over and sticks in the soil.

I guessed how difficult my selfishness would
Be when I heard the sound the hitch makes
When it slides off the drawbar onto the ground.

The Pistachio Nut

God crouches at night over a single pistachio.
The vastness of the Wind River Range in Wyoming
Has no more grandeur than the waist of a child.

Haydn tells us that we've inherited a mansion
On one of the Georgia sea islands. Then the last
Note burns down the courthouse and all the records.

Everyone who presses down the strings with his own fingers
Is on his way to Heaven; the pain in the fingertips
Goes toward healing the crimes the hands have done.

Let's give up the notion that great music is a way
Of praising human beings. It's good to agree that one drop
Of ocean water holds all of Kierkegaard's prayers.

When I hear the sitar give out the story of its life,
I know it is telling me how to behave—while kissing
The dear one's feet, to weep over my wasted life.

Robert, this poem will soon be over; and you
Are like a twig trembling on the lip of the falls.
Like a note of music, you are about to become nothing.

Listening to Old Music

The Rudra Vina

I don't know what would bring me closer to you.
Maybe slowing down this music, maybe waking
In the middle of the night, maybe diving for the bottom.

Maybe silence. The speed of the soul leaping over fences
Brings the toe forward. At other times, a book resting
On my chest takes me backward into my mother's arms.

The ache in the fold of my arm must be the old
Sadness that the newborn feels when he senses
That his father has come to claim him for this world.

Don't ask me whether to take Plato's side
Or Freud's. Just come over here and help me
Burn my books so we can move to Argentina.

The drum insists that the night we die
Will be a long night. The Rudra Vina goes on
Insisting that there is not enough suffering.

Well, music, go on growling about God.
I am rubbing my big face against my little face,
I am a blackbird flying through the night.

for Wesley and Sunil

Hiding in a Drop of Water

It is early morning, and death has forgotten us for
A while. Darkness owns the house, but I am alive.
I am ready to praise all the great musicians.

Whatever happens to me will also happen to you.
Surely you must have realized this from hearing
The way the strings cry out no matter who hits them.

From the great oak trees in the yard in October,
Leaves fall for hours every morning. Every night
A thousand wrinkled faces look up at the stars.

When Rabia's donkey fell dead in the desert, she shouted
To God, "Is that the way you treat an old woman?"
The donkey stood up, and they went on to the Meeting.

It is this reaching toward the Kaaba that keeps us glad.
It is this way of hiding inside a drop of water
That lets the hidden face become visible to everyone.

Gautama said that when the Great Ferris Wheel
Stops turning, you will still be way up
There, swinging in your seat and laughing.

Listening to Shahram Nazeri

I know the horses keep galloping for miles.
I know the ants keep lifting their feelers to heaven
And planning new triumphs, but it's already too late!

When Nazeri sings, I don't care if the Second
Adam comes down or not; I don't care if my words
Get you to cry or not—it's already too late!

The smell of coffee spreads out from the fire.
The wild-haired old women sing over the coffin.
Go on complaining and praying. It's already too late!

I know sweet vowels and inescapable rhythms.
I know how sweet it is when a young woman is here
And the old men think of God; but it's already too late!

My tongue never becomes bitter because my mouth
Keeps holding the grief pipe between my teeth.
Go on and conquer bitterness; it's already too late!

Here I am; I am all alone. It's early morning.
I am so happy. How can so much grandeur
Live beneath my skin? Go on asking; it's already too late!

Mailing Evidence to the Prosecutors

Every leaf in a storm points in the same direction.
The story of an affair is the story of our life.
The lover's body always tilts toward earth.

Lovers sometimes hide things under their pillows.
During our first year, we saved maps of Bali,
The Boundary Waters, and the Maltese lowlands.

We didn't know enough to move into a house.
We slept out in the barley fields night after night,
Watching the stars go over the edge of the world.

We know that lovers travel to distant countries,
Sometimes before they meet. We have agreed
We knew each other a hundred years ago.

When we had mailed evidence to the prosecutors
Three times, they understood that we were destined
For prison. When judges saw us coming, they clapped.

The two of us were blind, but we did drive our horses
Over the endless prairie. You judges, tell me
If you've ever seen wagons that traveled so far.

Waking in the Middle of the Night

I want to be true to what I have heard. It was
So sweet to hear music last night. There is so
Much joy in being afraid of the world together.

The snow in the branches, the sadness in your hands,
The foot tracks in the mud, the old Inca faces,
The trout who wait all year for the acorns to descend.

The sitar player is so much like the crow, who rises
Each morning in the sky above the black branches
And cries six cries with no memory of the light.

Every musician wants his fingers to play faster
So that he can go deeper into the kingdom of pain.
Each note on the string calls for one note more.

The hand that has written all these sounds down
Is like a bird who wakes in the middle of the night
And starts out toward its old nest on the mountain.

Robert, I don't know why you would have such
Good luck these days. Those lines about the crows
Crying are better than a whole night of sleep.

A Week in Florence

The donkey has led us through so many cultures!
Virgin after virgin has been born! Fra Lippi's voice
Is one ray of light coming down on the suffering.

Clams have survived so many long nights alone.
Why shouldn't Giotto stand for hours in his workshop?
Go ahead; fast in the night, and weep at dawn.

The green Arno carries the green blood of insects.
Angry men in the Baptistry have stabbed each
Other long before Dante went away weeping.

Mary's face shines so sweetly. Why? The hair
Of the Paleolithic elephants falls only once over
Their girlish eyes; then they enter eternal darkness.

The young woman is studying and praying in a room
Open to the Tuscan air. But the wide wings
Of the angel do not fit all the way inside the house.

Robert, you don't need to gaze through the window
To glimpse an angel. It's enough if you can see
Even one brown donkey's ear that Giotto painted.

for Mary and Alessandro

Rameau's Music

It is such a joy to hear Rameau's music when the night
Is just retreating from the oaky branches,
And the sun's enemy is throwing down his gloves.

Last night I wept so long and deeply in my dream
Because the fish were not returning to that bend
In the river where I swam so often as a boy.

Seeing that Jacob and Esau were both standing
By their father's bed, the old fisherman sent hooks down
And pulled the reckless boy up into the heavens.

Some music is as beautiful as snow on twigs.
I don't really see much distinction between
Words and the bow being drawn over the cello.

Well, how shall we complain after that?
We've been warned that what we receive on earth
Is smoke, fire, wind, mud, and darkness.

It's all right to balance on top of a pole! People
Say if you want the magic thing hidden from all
Others, you'll have to have a life full of exultation!

Losing the House in a Card Game

We have gambled, we've staked our house on a throw,
Lost a thousand times. Each time we finish the course,
We ride our horse back to the loser's circle.

We will never get tired of longing for good things
For each other. We are each, as we make love,
Like the mother bringing her child to the door of the school.

We were only fourteen when I saw you in Geometry
Class. We gobbled ecstasy; but we knew so little
About the skirts of glory stirring up the night.

This lovers' grief must be something the ancients
Worried about, because they knew that light
Of any kind can easily get lost in the dark clouds.

Oh Seth and Shem! Are you still grieving over
The seed of light that descended with no
Defender near into the Egypt of Mary's womb?

It's possible that we have nothing to mourn for,
Nothing to grieve over. We too, with every
Loss, have gone a little farther into Egypt.

A History of Mourning

It's odd that evening is so speckled with grief.
Birds start singing when the branch reddens.
But we write our poems when the sun goes down.

Our ancestors knew how to cry at death; but they
Had enough to do finding big stones to cover
The dead, and begetting new souls to replace them.

We slept on the limestone plains, and woke
Night after night, tracing the route the dead take
Through holes in limestone and on into the stars.

Some hands outlined with blown powder
On the walls of the cave have missing fingers.
We drew maps of the night sky in the dust.

How slowly it all went! One day a woman wept
When she saw a bone reddened with ochre.
A thousand years later, we put a bead in a grave.

Some graves stand among woods. We still don't
Understand why a pine coffin is so beautiful.
We are still brooding over why the sun rises.

Sand Heaps

Last night we took off our wolf skins, and danced
For hours, stomping our feet on the old rug. We were
Sand heaps breaking up in someone else's hands.

It was when we sang the same four bars over
And over that we gradually went mad
On one precious foot that was never put down.

We couldn't tell for a while where the door was
Or where the corners were. We didn't know if it was
Our crying or someone else's that filled the room.

What good will all this dancing do for anyone?
Oh, it's nothing; it will never do any good.
It's as precious as a hundred hours of prayer.

We have no idea why our bodies are jumping
Up and down, nor why our throats are full of sound.
All our years of everything have come to nothing.

We couldn't tell where the walls and floor were.
We lost all our certainty as we danced in the heat.
All our years of everything have come to this.

The Dingy Playing Cards

Friends, it's time to give up our hope for Rapture.
Saucers will not carry us away. Raskolnikov
Had to depend on the police to help him sleep.

Our soul loves the dingy cards that have been dealt
To the ne'er-do-wells. The old men put the old
Queens down with their smoke-stained fingers.

In the Cirque du Soleil, when the acrobats
Sweep out over the crowd, babies are being
Born who know much more than we ever did.

The yellow teeth of old jackrabbits explains a lot
About the shortage of mercy; the caterpillar's walk
Reminds us of the Mongols galloping toward Khorakhan.

After the funeral, once they are safe, the dead begin
To miss losing at cards. We know that Cain and Abel
Want to meet each other again on the plowed field.

Robert, there's not a single humiliation we could
Have done without. We are still perched on a pole.
What will happen to us depends a lot on the wind.

The Fat Old Couple Whirling Around

The drum says that the night we die will be a long night.
It says the children have time to play. Tell the grownups
They can pull the curtains around the bed tonight.

The old man wants to know how the war ended.
The young girl wants her breasts to cause the sun to rise.
The thinker wants to keep misunderstanding alive.

It's all right if the earthly monk is buried near the altar.
It's all right if the singer fails to turn up for her concert.
It's good if the fat old couple keeps whirling around.

Let the parents sing over the cradle every night.
Let the pelicans go on living in their stickly nests.
Let the duck go on loving the mud around her feet.

It's all right if the ant always remembers his way home.
It's all right if Bach keeps reaching for the same note.
It's all right if we knock the ladder away from the house.

Even if you are a puritan it would be all right
If you join the lovers in their ruined house tonight.
It's good if you become a soul and then disappear.

Shabistari and *The Secret Garden*

I can't stop praising Shabistari for bringing
The gnat's and the elephant's legs close to each other.
Next I want Sunday to be brought closer to Monday.

Suppose a bit of straw were able to marry the wind.
Haven't you noticed those good marriages when
The wind and the chaff go down the road together?

When a poem takes me to that place where
No story ever happens twice, all I want
Is a warm room, and a thousand years of thought.

Conrad said the dark swimmer did reach his ship.
If we sink into the suffering that's right for us,
Our dreams will have all that Adam and Eve wept for.

Amazing things do happen. One morning Kierkegaard
Explains exactly what *ressentiment* is
And the mouse agrees to marry everyone in the room.

Robert, those high spirits don't prove you are
A close friend of truth; but they do suggest
That you have loved *The Secret Garden*.

The Night the Cities Burned

It must have been Saturn and the other old men
Who arranged this night of darkness for us.
So much of our life goes by in the murky dark.

When you open an apple in order to take in
Its sweet fruit, be sure to eat the tiny black seeds
So you can taste the tartness that Swift knew.

I'm never tired of despair and desperation,
And I won't be quiet. I keep crying out that the house
Is being robbed. I want even the thieves to know.

We'll have to help each other to hear, because
It was in the middle of the night during a storm
That Sophocles and all the weepers were born.

We've tried to go straight for a hundred years
With the help of reason. Friends, we are tufted
Nuthatches blown for miles in the dawn wind.

I don't know why these poems keep veering off
Toward darkness. Robert, you are actually a daughter
Of Lot, fleeing from the ruins of the Enlightenment.

 for Michael Ventura

The Bridegroom

The bridegroom wanted to reach the Norwegian Church.
But the roads were made impassable by huge snows.
We are each the Bridegroom longing for existence.

Marriage brings the moth close to the candleflame.
With their frail wings, men and women
Are constantly flying into the fire of existence.

Some say that each drop of groundwater in Kansas
Knows about the ocean. How can this be?
Every drop of water longs like us for existence.

Abu Sa'id fasted in the desert for twenty years.
Later when he came back, his dragon friend
Wept. "Your suffering gave me a hint of existence."

When the pianist's fingers strike all the notes
In the Tenth Prelude, it's clear Bach's soul has been
Leaping about like a hare in the field of existence.

Robert, you're close to joy but not quite there.
You are a hunchback standing in an Italian
Square, looking in at the festival of existence.

The Head of Barley

I don't know if you've ever met a head of barley
In late August, protected by its spiky beards.
It sticks to your clothes from pure faithfulness.

When a farm girl picks up a Leghorn feather
And waves it in an empty barn, the storm it
Raises is as subtle as the wind of faithfulness.

The last maple leaf hanging on its tree against
The blue sky is like that angel who brought
His wing-tips in near Mary's faithfulness.

The sitar player keeps track of twelve notes
For each raga, five up and seven down. Even
With twelve brides, he maintains faithfulness.

You know a needle sticks up for itself; it's
Not a generous thing, but, joining with the hand,
It starts out on the road to faithfulness.

It's hard to know what to say about the marvels
Inside the soul. Even those of us who have broken
Many promises can still hope for faithfulness.

Adam's Understanding

Adam agreed the ocean would be the home of salt.
We all understood our souls would hang by a thread.
God agreed the pearl would be out of our hands.

What did the Prodigal Son find inside his room?
His boots and sword, a tiny monkey chained
To an iron ball, a bed, and forgetfulness.

I have written poems lying in so many small beds.
Sometimes a cross hangs on the inside of the door.
Mostly the dark of early dawn is in the room.

Some say farmers have taken on themselves the crime
Of saving and sowing wheat; and bakers have taken
On themselves the crime of baking the bread!

This is what I say, "I want what's owed to me."
A voice says, "We have our inheritance."
Whose voice is that? Is that my old teacher?

Oh what a glory it is that the winter snow
Should be so deep, that we know so little,
And the future should be out of our hands!

Eating Blackberry Jam

When I hear that we all belong to nonexistence,
I drop my eyes, but then I raise them out
Of love for the little creatures of nonexistence.

Some say that perch became like each other
To keep the shark from zeroing in. But staying alive
Doesn't mean they are free from nonexistence.

The cries of the infant barn-swallows rising from
The mud-nests fastened ingeniously to the rafters
Taught me to love the skinny birds of nonexistence.

Taoists with their thin beards fishing all day
With a straight hook tell us they have learned
Not to expect a whole lot from nonexistence.

Blackberries have so many faces that their jam
Is a kind of thickening of nothing; each of us
Loves to eat the thick syrup of nonexistence.

When each stanza closes with the same word,
I am glad. A friend says, "If you're proud of that,
You must be one of the secretaries of nonexistence!"

The Buff-Chested Grouse

I have spent my whole life doing what I love.
Let's honor the quail who searches so hard for food.
Here I am, playing flute in a cistern like Joseph.

My genius amounts to persistence in following
Elephants through the wind. Sometimes the long vowels
Go on ahead and show us where the road is.

Thank God for Jaufre Rudel who taught even
The Vikings the road of love. We are incompetent, hopeless
Lovers, but we do play the shawm in the wind.

It was only when I was out in the fields, hiding
From the winds, that I understood that what fell
To pieces last night could be whole this morning.

I don't know if you've heard the buff-chested grouse
When he drums on an old log. He is like Hafez
Repeating something he has heard from his teacher.

Robert, I hope you're not bragging in this poem.
Don't drag out the comparison to Joseph.
We're just talking here of feathers blown in the wind.

Stealing Sugar from the Castle

We are poor students who stay after school to study joy.
We are like those birds in the India mountains.
I am a widow whose child is her only joy.

The only thing I hold in my ant-like head
Is the builder's plan of the castle of sugar.
Just to steal one grain of sugar is a joy!

Like a bird, we fly out of darkness into the hall,
Which is lit with singing, then fly out again.
Being shut out of the warm hall is also a joy.

I am a laggard, a loafer, and an idiot. But I love
To read about those who caught one glimpse
Of the Face, and died twenty years later in joy.

I don't mind your saying I will die soon.
Even in the sound of the word *soon*, I hear
The word *you* which begins every sentence of joy.

"You're a thief!" the judge said. "Let's see
Your hands!" I showed my callused hands in court.
My sentence was a thousand years of joy.

TALKING INTO THE EAR OF A DONKEY

2011

Ravens Hiding in a Shoe

There is something men and women living in houses
Don't understand. The old alchemists standing
Near their stoves hinted at it a thousand times.

Ravens at night hide in an old woman's shoe.
A four-year-old speaks some ancient language.
We have lived our own death a thousand times.

Each sentence we speak to friends means the opposite
As well. Each time we say, "I trust in God," it means
God has already abandoned us a thousand times.

Mothers again and again have knelt in church
In wartime asking God to protect their sons,
And their prayers were refused a thousand times.

The baby loon follows the mother's sleek
Body for months. By the end of summer, she
Has dipped her head into Rainy Lake a thousand times.

Robert, you've wasted so much of your life
Sitting indoors to write poems. Would you
Do that again? I would, a thousand times.

Keeping Our Small Boat Afloat

So many blessings have been given to us
During the first distribution of light, that we are
Admired in a thousand galaxies for our grief.

Don't expect us to appreciate creation or to
Avoid mistakes. Each of us is a latecomer
To the earth, picking up wood for the fire.

Every night another beam of light slips out
From the oyster's closed eye. So don't give up hope
That the door of mercy may still be open.

Seth and Shem, tell me, are you still grieving
Over the spark of light that descended with no
Defender near into the Egypt of Mary's womb?

It's hard to grasp how much generosity
Is involved in letting us go on breathing,
When we contribute nothing valuable but our grief.

Each of us deserves to be forgiven, if only for
Our persistence in keeping our small boat afloat
When so many have gone down in the storm.

Longing for the Acrobat

There is so much sweetness in children's voices,
And so much discontent at the end of day,
And so much satisfaction when a train goes by.

I don't know why the rooster keeps on crying,
Nor why the elephant lifts his knobby trunk,
Nor why Hawthorne kept hearing trains at night.

A handsome child is a gift from God,
And a friend is a vein in the back of the hand,
And a wound is an inheritance from the wind.

Some say we are living at the end of time,
But I believe a thousand pagan ministers
Will arrive tomorrow to baptize the wind.

There's nothing we need to do about Saint John.
Whenever he laid his hands on earth
The well water was sweet for a hundred miles.

Everywhere people are longing for a deeper life.
Let's hope some acrobat will come by
And give us a hint how to get into heaven.

Nirmala's Music

The music that Nirmala is playing today goes
By two names: The One Who Finds Lost Things,
And The One Through Whom Everything Is Lost.

Tigers go on eating people in the Forest
Of Existence. The gods agree to this. Saints
Admire whiskers that have been dipped in blood.

Women with their newly washed hair, the souls
Born again and again into sleek, fresh bodies,
Boards leaning against a barn . . . what does it all mean?

Men think ahead, and are mainly providential.
They laid out Egypt. But I like women so much.
They say: "Let the lambs come and be killed."

And women suffer the most. Between every child born,
So many rugs are woven and taken apart. The water
Of a hundred bowls is poured out on the ground.

The hungry tigers follow the disappearing dogs
Into the woods of life. Women understand this,
For this is a world in which everything is lost.

for Nirmala Rajasekar

The Frogs After Dark

I am so much in love with mournful music
That I don't bother to look for violinists.
The aging peepers satisfy me for hours.

The ant moves on his tiny Sephardic feet.
The flute is always glad to repeat the same note.
The ocean rejoices in its dusky mansion.

Bears are often piled up close to each other.
In caves of bears, it's just one hump
After another, and there is no one to sort it out.

You and I have spent so many hours working.
We have paid dearly for the life we have.
It's all right if we do nothing tonight.

We've heard the fiddlers tuning their old fiddles,
And the singer urging the low notes to come.
We've heard her trying to keep the dawn from breaking.

There is some slowness in life that is right for us.
But we love to remember the way the soul leaps
Over and over into the lonely heavens.

The Sympathies of the Long Married

Oh well, let's go on eating the grains of eternity.
What do we care about improvements in travel?
Angels sometimes cross the river on old turtles.

Shall we worry about who gets left behind?
That one bird flying through the clouds is enough.
Your sweet face at the door of the house is enough.

The two farm horses stubbornly pull the wagon.
The mad crows carry away the tablecloth.
Most of the time, we live through the night.

Let's not drive the wild angels from our door.
Maybe the mad fields of grain will move.
Maybe the troubled rocks will learn to walk.

It's all right if we're troubled by the night.
It's all right if we can't recall our own name.
It's all right if this rough music keeps on playing.

I've given up worrying about men living alone.
I do worry about the couple who live next door.
Some words heard through the screen door are enough.

The Roof Nail

A hundred boats are still looking for shore.
There is more in my hopes than I imagined.
The tiny roof nail lies on the ground, aching for the roof.
Some little bone in our foot is longing for heaven.

Dealing with Parents

It's hard to know what to say about parents:
One man said, "I failed my parents." He led his parents
Across a lousy street—two lines of traffic.
Another started a lost colony for his parents.
He rowed across the river, towing his parents.
He bought them boots and pith helmets,
And sent them into battle. One man dressed them
In Austrian uniforms and gave them
Maps of Russia. No one ever saw them again.
Another man who had studied alchemy
Tried to transubstantiate his parents. It used
A lot of heat but there wasn't much change.
Someone else I knew stored his parents
In an empty cistern—the ladder is still sticking out.
Another man tied his parents all one day
And night in a rocking chair. And they
Died all right. . . . But by the end, they
Knew for certain that they'd had children.

The Old Fishing Lines

Sometimes I get in my car on a late October day
And drive north. Everything that I haven't done—
Raking, visiting—all those reasons for not living—
Fall away. I pass half-abandoned summer towns,
Admiring the shadows thrown by bare trees
On bare lakes where cold waves lap the sand.

The renegade minister—the one they all gossip
About—would see those waves too, after throwing
His Sunday hat out the window. He'll be
All right. Death hugs the underside of oak leaves.
In each cove you pass you will see
What you had to say no to once.

It's all right if you walk down to the shore.
You'll feel time passing, the way the summer has.
You'll see the little holes that raindrops leave in fine sand
And the old fishing lines driven up on the rocks.

Starting a Poem

You're alone. Then there's a knock
On the door. It's a word. You
Bring it in. Things go
OK for a while. But this word

Has relatives. Soon
They turn up. None of them work.
They sleep on the floor, and they steal
Your tennis shoes.

You started it; you weren't
Content to leave things alone.
Now the den is a mess, and the
Remote is gone.

That's what being married
Is like! You never receive your
Wife only, but the
Madness of her family.

Now see what's happened?
Where is your car? You won't
Be able to find
The keys for a week.

I Have Daughters and I Have Sons

1

Who is out there at six a.m.? The man
Throwing newspapers onto the porch,
And the roaming souls suddenly
Drawn down into their sleeping bodies.

2

Wild words of Jacob Böhme
Go on praising the human body,
But heavy words of the ascetics
Sway in the fall gales.

3

Do I have a right to my poems?
To my jokes? To my loves?
Oh foolish man, knowing nothing—
Less than nothing—about desire.

4

I have daughters and I have sons.
When one of them lays a hand
On my shoulder, shining fish
Turn suddenly in the deep sea.

5

At this age, I especially love dawn
On the sea, stars above the trees,
Pages in *The Threefold Life*,
And the pale faces of baby mice.

6

Perhaps our life is made of struts
And paper, like those early
Wright Brothers planes. Neighbors
Run along holding the wingtips.

7

I do love Yeats's fierceness
As he jumped into a poem,
And that lovely calm in my father's
Hands, as he buttoned his coat.

Wanting Sumptuous Heavens

No one grumbles among the oyster clans,
And lobsters play their bone guitars all summer.
Only we, with our opposable thumbs, want
Heaven to be, and God to come, again.
There is no end to our grumbling; we want
Comfortable earth and sumptuous heaven.
But the heron standing on one leg in the bog
Drinks his dark rum all day, and is content.

A Family Thing

I guess it's an old family
Thing. Someone is Napoleon,
Someone is sacrificed. Call in
Jesus, if you don't get it.

Pick up that cookie on the floor.
Let the hired man go on
Wasting his life. He'll find
Someone to waste it with.

It's like a game in which
The game itself loses.
It's like a picnic in which
The basket eats the food.

It's all right if I go to college;
Most people don't. It's all right
To end up bringing your own
Father home. Just be quiet.

Some powers are stronger
Than we are. They never say
When the battle is.
It was last night. You lost.

Keeping Quiet

A friend of mine says that every war
Is some violence in childhood coming closer.
Those whoppings in the shed weren't a joke.
On the whole, it didn't turn out well.

This has been going on for thousands
Of years! It doesn't change. Something
Happened to me, and I can't tell
Anyone, so it will happen to you.

Morning Pajamas

When you've slept all night in a warm bed, sometimes
You'll find a punky fragrance in your pajamas.
It's a bit lowlife, but satisfying.
It's some sort of companionable warmth
That your balls created during the night.
It's a mammal delight, related
To the cow's udder, one
Of the nouns of this earth.
Don't be ashamed, friends;
Don't throw your pajamas in the washer,
Don't open the window;
Forget the pilgrims!
Think how sweet it is
That knowledge should come
From a source so deep.

The Slim Fir Seeds

The nimble ovenbird, the dignity of pears,
The simplicity of oars, the imperishable
Engines inside slim fir seeds, all of these
Make clear how much we want the impermanent
To be permanent. We want the hermit wren
To keep her eggs even during the storm.
But that's impossible. We are perishable;
Friends, we are salty, impermanent kingdoms.

Tristan and Isolde

The glad body sings its four-leggéd tunes.
It has its honesty. Lovers know the obstinacy
Of the animal, the grunts that say to spirit,
Gone, gone! The awl pulls from the leather;
The thread pulls from the needle's eye. Later
He seems good to her eyes, like a waterhole
Muddied by animals. Tristan and Isolde
Love their bawdy lodge, no north, no south.

Turkish Pears in August

Sometimes a poem has her own husband
And children, her nooks and gardens and kitchens,
Her stairs, and those sweet-armed serving boys
Who carry veal in shiny copper pans.
Some poems do give plebeian sweets
Tastier than the chocolates French diners
Eat at evening, and old pleasures abundant
As Turkish pears picked in the garden in August.

Thoreau as a Lover

Dear old Thoreau abandoned his scandalous life
To live among the sand cranes and the ants.
He wasn't exactly a crowd-pleaser, but he
Kept company with his handsome language.
Each day he walked alone in the woods,
Bringing along a lover's book which told which flower
Was likely to blossom today. Well, well;
Beyond that, he lived extravagantly alone.

So Much Time

December's foolishness, embers fall, tempters
Fly up into the dreamt palace. Things move so
Slowly in the soul. It must be that we've
Already been grieving for a hundred years.
Old men and women know how much time
Can go by while praying. Let's not try
To cheer each other up. It's all right.
We can stay in grieving another hundred years.

The Grackles

Grackles stroll about on the black floor of sorrow.
Rabbis robed in saffron feed them
Minnow bread. . . . They come to meet you.
Moses and his black wife walk like birds
And dance. Among the stalks of timothy grass
The saddled horses drink from sorrow tanks.
But the grackles' toes are springy—they walk
Over the footprints the dreamer made last night.

For the Old Gnostics

The Fathers put their trust in the end of the world
And they were wrong. The Gnostics were right and not
Right. Dragons copulate with their knobby tails.
Some somnolent wealth rises unconcerned,
Yes, over there! Ponderous stubborn
Sorrow weighs down the flying Gospels.
Scholars cobble together new versions.
The untempered soul grumbles in empty light.

Silent in the Moonlight

Silent in the moonlight, no beginning or end.
Alone, and not alone. A man and a woman lie
On open ground, under an antelope robe.
They sleep under animal skin, looking up
At the old, clear stars. How many years?
The robe thrown over them, rough
Where they sleep. Outside, the moon, the plains
Silent in the moonlight, no beginning or end.

What Is Sorrow For?

What is sorrow for? It is a storehouse
Where we store wheat, barley, corn and tears.
We step to the door on a round stone,
And the storehouse feeds all the birds of sorrow.
And I say to myself: Will you have
Sorrow at last? Go on, be cheerful in autumn,
Be stoic, yes, be tranquil, calm;
Or in the valley of sorrows spread your wings.

The Camels

So many camels kneel to take their burdens on.
What choice do we have but to go down? How
Can I be close to you if I'm not sad? The clam tumbles
In the surf, and amber holds the secret desires
The bee felt before his room grew silent.
The salmon has to weave through so many waters
Before he can return to his old home.
So many stammerers labor to speak one word.

Limits

So in the bear's cabin we come to earth.
There are limits. Among all the limits
We know so few things. How is it I know
Only one river—its turns—and one woman?
The love of woman is the knowing of grief.
There are no limits to grief. The loving man
Simmers his porcupine stew. Among the tim-
Ber growing on earth grief finds roots.

The Housefly

Blessings now on all
Who bend their heads!
Didn't Joseph bend
His head low to kiss
The baker's feet?
The muskrat gives up
His father's house.
The housefly bends his
Head down and gives
Up his elegant
Heaven to live with us.

My Father at Forty

I loved him so much. I've said
That before, so don't be surprised.
It was a first love. Go ahead, open
Your hand. Do scissors beat
Paper? Does rock beat scissors?
It's just love and can't be
Explained. Probably it
Happened early. You're looking
At it. The way I found
Of opening a poem I took
From the way he walked into a field.

The Man at the Door

Last night in my dream I took some steps
Underground. It seemed to be a holy place—
Perhaps monks a thousand years ago
Thought there. I had almost forgotten them.

How could we forget? Well, it's easy.
A guard at the door—you know the kind,
Those who keep people out—stopped me.
I began singing, "Hum-du-lah,

"Hum-du-lah." I couldn't remember
What those words meant.
But the man at the door grew
Light-headed, and let me slip in.

The Hermit

Early in the morning the hermit wakes, hearing
The roots of the fir tree stir beneath his floor.
Someone is there. That strength buried
In earth carries up the summer world. When
A man loves a woman, he nourishes her.
Dancers strew the lawn with the light of their feet.
When a woman loves the earth, she nourishes it.
Earth nourishes what no one can see.

The Longing

I don't know why air drops gather on the inside
Of water glasses, and why the shaggy dog
Always seems to be waiting for heaven.

We have had more blessings than our parents had.
Even on Mondays, we can knock on doors
Asking strangers to give us a ticket to heaven.

The porcupine climbs straight up the tree
With his heavy tail hanging down,
But he doesn't give two beans for heaven.

The old man lying in bed writing poems
Feels his brain light up, and he knows
That in some odd way he is approaching heaven.

Men sometimes turn around to see a woman better.
The eyes of beautiful women often glow
When the handsome priest talks of heaven.

I write these poems so happily each day.
I guess it means that I've had a longing
All morning to write the word "heaven."

What Did We See Today?

Some days we are passive, listening to the incoming waves.
On other days, we are like a light that sweeps
Out over the husky soybean fields all night.

What did we see today? Horses at the end
Of their tethering ropes, the wing of affection going over,
Flying bulls glimpsed passing the moon disc.

Rather than arguing about whether Giordano Bruno
Was right or not, it might be better to fall silent
And lose ourselves in the curved energy.

We know how many men live alone in their twenties,
And how many women are married to the wrong person,
And how many fathers and sons are strangers to each other.

It's all right if we keep forgetting the way home.
It's all right if we don't remember when we were born.
It's all right if we write the same poem over and over.

Robert, I don't know why you talk so confidently
About yourself in this way. There are a lot of shady
Characters in this town, and you are one of them.

The Hawk in His Nest

It's all right if this suffering goes on for years.
It's all right if the hawk never finds his own nest.
It's all right if we never receive the love we want.

It's all right if we listen to the sitar for hours.
It doesn't matter how softly the musician plays.
Sooner or later the melody will say it all.

It doesn't matter if we regret our crimes or not.
The mice will carry our defeats into Asia,
And the Tuvan throat-singers will tell the whole story.

It's all right if we can't remain cheerful all day.
The task we have accepted is to go down
To renew our friendship with the ruined things.

It's all right if people think we are idiots.
It's all right if we lie face down on the earth.
It's all right if we open the coffin and climb in.

It's not our fault that things have gone wrong.
Let's agree that it was Saturn and the other old men
Who have arranged this series of defeats for us.

Smoke-Stained Fingers

There is still time for the old days when the musician
Stayed inside his bubble of joy, and the old men
Threw cards down with their smoke-stained fingers.

Let's hope Brooklyn Bridge will remain standing,
That Jacob marries either Rachel or Leah,
And the Appalachians don't wear all the way down.

No one minds if we are scruffy and badly dressed.
The old man who is checking names at the door
Speaks only Hungarian, and is blind as well.

There's no telling how many hours are left to us.
The plateaus in New Mexico lift a little each year.
It's like hearing a dog barking from far away.

Some birdcalls come straight through the walls.
I don't know why we bother to listen to them
When we've never heard our own cries.

Don't give up, friends. Somewhere inside us,
Jacob is tending sheep on our old farm.
The angels are still sending messages to Joseph.

What the Old Poets Failed to Say

The sunlight on wheat heads in August holds me firmly,
For I am in love with the wheat soon to be cut.
Let's thank whoever it was who kept sorrow alive.

Tell me who brought Hafez out of the grave.
Who brings us news of the Thirtieth Kingdom?
I can't stop clapping my hands over this question.

Even though we know God lays our head
On the block, we thank him for it all, and we
Remember the loving we have enjoyed at night.

Tell me why the suffering of the violin string
Goes on for years, why the coyote calls at night,
And why the bird never settles down on one branch.

Tell me why my titles are often so sad,
And why cattle keep on going every day
To the slaughterhouse, and why wars go on so long.

Night after night goes by in the old man's head.
We try to ask new questions. But whatever
The old poets failed to say will never be said.

NEW POEMS

2012–2013

———————————————————————————

Plan for a Year

Suppose that for a year we wrote poems only
About men and women whose lives had failed.
We wouldn't have to stop writing about
Ourselves—that's one good thing. But

We'd have to give up bringing Cezanne
Into the poems, and cut way back on Dickinson.
There'd be fewer mentions of Eckhart and none
About those saints banished by the Church.

But we could go on writing about butterflies
Setting out over the Pacific, and those immigrant
Women in log cabins playing Haydn,
And we could talk about what happened to God.

Harmonium

I've loved this blue book of poems for forty years.
A man wrote it, but his mother is in it. She's
Present in that wisp of feeling that rises, all at once—
Those frail instants that hard-pressed men ignore.

Of course he has a lot of derring-do,
And bravado, jokes about Cotton Mather
And Abraham Lincoln, but the best lines are really
Fleeting details that women mainly notice.

It's hard to know what to say about this. Some men glance
At the world but then back to the blue flower
Usually ignored, like that moment in courting:
The secret moment out of which forty years is born.

Tomas Tranströmer and the Human Ear

Somewhere there's a rock pile in a field.
Some trees grow between the rocks.
Farmers learn to plow around it.
It's a power generator for silence.

When this man lifts his sly, amused eyes
Some new sort of speech appears on the paper.
One equation makes the Pacific trenches
Equal to the porches of the human ear.

Sometimes a spy passes a blank paper
Alone in his room through the Solution.
His poems resemble the way Euclid
Found the solution to the Third Theorem.

My Father at Dawn

Is my father still working with the cows?
They rattle their stanchions, waiting for the silage.
The calves are waiting, and the pigs grunting.
Horses stamp their hooves in the dusty stalls.

While it's still dark, my father gets up, puts on
His overalls, puts on his stubborn life,
Which he stubbornly cherishes—it is *in*
Him just as the call of the dove inheres

In every cell of her body. The life he had chosen
Was what he longed for. That's what we think.
Meanwhile the cows are waiting,
And the horses are restless in their stalls.

Love of the Wind

We've spent a lot of time keeping some old men alive.
I don't think you should criticize us for that.
Even old sailors keep their love of the wind.

We know so little of our neighbor's sorrow.
He never told us what happened to his son.
What can it mean that Jesus had no sister?

We'll never know anything better than a dog.
It doesn't matter how deeply he sleeps.
The sleeping dog leaves all the world for the floor.

It's all right if the family comes together at night
And sings like sailors when the wind rises.
The roof of the house will last the night.

I've never been an old friend to the wind.
Don't expect me to be happy about haystacks
Scattered in a storm or blown-down barns.

A few homely details are enough for us.
We're tired of complaining of life and death.
Even old sailors keep their love of the wind.

It Takes a Long Time

Let the insects go on shouting their hallelujahs;
Let the crickets go on hiding their parents;
Let the goats complain they can't find Jerusalem.

Eternity waits for the moose to start moving.
The mouse keeps circling around for its own tail.
Finally it just curls up and goes to sleep.

We know how long it takes to make a waterfall,
How many years the oak tree waits in the orchard,
How long the caterpillar takes to wash his feet.

The sitarist's head bends over the skinny sitar.
Notes come in from a hundred Indian villages.
The long notes sweeten the sea bottom.

It will be years before the great dragon returns.
Meanwhile, our grandmother has a lot to do,
And the tired birds keep flying over the ocean.

It will be years before the busy sea calms down,
And the wind stops blowing ships landward,
And the goats give up looking for Jerusalem.

Listening to Monteverdi

I come from a long line of Protestant revolutionaries
Who refused the old marriages with Rome,
But I'm still hoping to sit at Moses' side.

Every night the old angels call to us,
Promising good things. For centuries the oysters
Have been opening and closing at Moses' side.

For centuries I have been no one at all, tossed
Up and down, a wild bird in the storm, and yet all
That time I have been sitting at Moses' side.

How can it be that we are sons and daughters
Of Danish tribesmen, barely Christian at all,
Yet all this time we have been sitting at Moses's side.

We know how easily we can veer off the road,
And get stuck in the snow, though all that time
We still imagine we are sitting at Moses' side.

Let's forget the idea that we are the old ones, chosen
To carry the creation. We are all latecomers
To the earth, still hoping to sit at Moses' side.

It's Not to Worry

Don't worry, friends. This night of drinking will not
Keep you from your wedding. Each of us has been
Sent out, as Hafez said, naked on the roads!

You've been putting sumptuous images in poems
For years, hoping they will keep you warm,
But they don't. You're still naked on the roads!

People used to believe that only the heavy drinkers
Were badly dressed. Now all of us
Are wandering around naked on the roads!

Some of our old teachers used to wear vests
With gold chains and watch fobs. Now look
At them: all of them are naked on the roads!

The wild Italians like St. Francis had a sense
Of it—take a year off, get rid of your clothes,
Pick up a stick and go naked on the roads!

Sometimes it's good to fail and be stupid.
If Hafez hadn't been stupid, he wouldn't have had
The joy of being naked on the roads!

Index

Index

Index

Index